Kaizen Express

Fundamentals for Your Lean Journey

by Toshiko Narusawa *and* John Shook

Foreword by Jim Womack

The Lean Enterprise Institute
Cambridge, MA, USA
lean.org

March 2009

ISBN: 978-1-934109-23-6
Cover design by Off-Piste Design, Inc.
March 2009

The Lean Enterprise Institute, Inc.
One Cambridge Center, Cambridge, MA 02142 USA
Tel: 617-871-2900 • Fax: 617-871-2999 • lean.org

Also by Toshiko Narusawa

Learning to See: Value-Stream Mapping to Create Value and Eliminate Muda
(Japanese translation)

Creating Level Pull: A Lean Production-System Improvement Guide for Production-Control, Operations, and Engineering Professionals
(Japanese translation)

Also by John Shook

Learning to See: Value-Stream Mapping to Create Value and Eliminate Muda
(co-authored with Mike Rother)

Managing to Learn: Using the A3 Management Process to Solve Problems, Gain Agreement, Mentor, and Lead

序文

リーンの手法や基本的な考え方についての本なら、今や大量に存在します。しかし、ありとあらゆる領域についての教材が潤沢にあるがゆえに、かえって道に迷い、何をなすべきかを考えるのに時間を浪費してしまうこともまたありがちです。リーンなマネジメントや戦略、企業文化といったハイレベルなことばかりに心を奪われて、本当に仕事がなされているレベルでしっかりした基盤を築くことを完全に無視している企業に私は頻繁に出会っています。

そのようなわけで、トヨタ生産方式(TPS)の原則と、継続的改善を通してロジカルな順序でそれらの原則を現場で具現化する方法を簡潔に描いた1冊の本を持って成沢俊子とジョン・シュックがLEIにアプローチしてきたとき、私はうれしく思いました。それに、私はトヨタで工夫されてきたオリジナルの日本製TPS教材のスタイルを大好きになっていましたから、その本がシンプルなマンガを使って描かれていたことも好ましく感じました。実際、図で見せることは何千語にも相当する価値があり、それらの図はTPSを築いてきた人々の精神を継ぐものです。

成沢は、日本の大きなエレクトロニクス企業NECで20年近くTPSリーダーとして働きながら、また後には東アジアのさまざまな企業でTPSトレーナーとして働きながら、改善を通してTPSを学びました。ずいぶん昔のことですが、彼女はNECの改善を私に紹介してくれたことがあります。そのとき私は、彼女には教える才能があるとすぐに分かりました。

一方、ジョン・シュックは1983年からTPSを日本の外の世界へ向けて説明してきました。バリュー・ストリーム・マッピングを解説した、すでに古典と言い得る彼の著作*Learning to See*は13ヶ国語に翻訳され(日本語への翻訳は成沢)、今までに50万部以上売れています。また、彼の近著*Managing to Learn*は、リーン・マネジメントとリーン・リーダーシップを扱った意欲作です。二人とも世界のあちこちで改善を成功させてきた確かな実績を持っており、その二人が組んだチームです。読者は安心してよろしい。

読者の皆さんが皆さん自身のカイゼン・エクスプレスを発進させるためには一連のコンセプトとツールを一定の論理的な順序に従って実践していく必要がありますが、著者らは簡潔にまとめた本書のなかで、それらのコンセプトとツールを順序立てています。著者らは質問形式を用いてそれを描きます。これは、あなたとあなたの仲間がこれから出会うことになる多くの障害や課題を解決するのに、たいへんに役立つはずです。

人生は常に複雑で、単純明快さは希少かつ喜ばしいものですから、私たちは本書に大きな期待を抱いています。しかしまた、本書をより良くするためには皆さんからのフィードバックが必要です。皆さんの経験、成功、そして失敗を、どうぞkaizenexpress@lean.orgへ寄せてください。世界は今こそもっと改善が必要です。この小さな一冊は、快速改善の道を行く確かなガイドになるでしょう。

ジム・ウォマック
リーン・エンタープライズ・インスティテュート　創立者・会長
マサチューセッツ州ケンブリッジ
2009年3月

Foreword

There is now a vast literature of lean methods and principles. But the wide array of materials makes it easy to get lost and waste time pondering just what to do. In addition, it's easy to forget the fundamentals while pursuing advanced methods. I constantly encounter firms focusing on high-level issues of lean management, strategy, and corporate culture that have completely ignored creating a solid foundation at the level where the real work is done.

I was therefore delighted when Toshiko Narusawa and John Shook approached LEI with a volume designed to quickly explain the principles of the Toyota Production System (TPS) and how to implement them in the gemba in a logical sequence through continuous kaizen. And I was equally delighted that the material is presented in the simple, cartoon style I've grown to love in the original Japanese work on TPS developed at Toyota. Pictures really are worth thousands of words and these pictures are in the spirit of the founders of TPS.

Ms. Narusawa has come by her TPS knowledge the hard way, through innumerable kaizen during nearly two decades as a TPS leader in Japanese electronics giant NEC and recently as a TPS trainer for many major firms in East Asia. Many years ago she took me through improvement activities inside NEC and I knew instantly that she has the gift for teaching TPS.

John Shook, over the same time period, beginning in 1983, has explained TPS to the world outside Japan. His classic explanation of value-stream mapping, *Learning to See* (translated into Japanese by Ms. Narusawa), has sold more than half a million copies in thirteen languages, and his recent *Managing to Learn* takes on the challenge of lean management and leadership. Together your authors are a highly experienced team with a record of kaizen success around the world. You are in good hands.

In this brief volume the authors sequence the concepts and tools you will need to launch your own kaizen express, putting them in a logical order. They do this using a question-and-answer format that will help you and your colleagues remove the most common barriers and challenges.

Because life is complicated and simplicity is rare and precious, we have high hopes for this volume. But we need your feedback to continue improving it. So we hope we will hear about your experience, successes, and failures at kaizenexpress@lean.org. The world needs more kaizen now and this little volume is surely a helpful guide on the path to high-speed improvement.

Jim Womack
Founder and Chairman
Lean Enterprise Institute
Cambridge, MA
March 2009

はじめに

“Kaizen”という言葉は、日本語を飛び出して世界中で使われるようになりました。世界的に使われるようになった用語というものは、もはや翻訳する必要はなく、多くの人々にとって様々な意味を持つに至ります。本書カイゼン・エクスプレスで、私たちは、一人ひとりとチームのレベルでの実践を通した学びを大切にしながら、同時に基本にたちかえるというアプローチを描きます。このアプローチの基盤をなす基本的なスキル、行動のしかた、そしてツールが存在するという事実をあいまいにしたまま、多くの人々が理論に集中してカイゼン意識を取り込もうと努力しています。カイゼン・エクスプレスは、トヨタ生産方式(TPS)の考え方は実践を通して体得する他なく、「行動のしかたを新しいものに変えようと考えるより、考え方を新しいものに変えるように自身の行動を変えることのほうが容易である」という信念に立脚します。

本書は、もともと、TPSを学ぶための日英対訳のワンセットの教材として開発されたものです。はじめ、2005年から2007年にかけて日本の月刊誌・工場管理(日刊工業新聞社)に連載され、後に単行本「英語でkaizen！　トヨタ生産方式　Kaizen Express」(同社刊)にまとめられました。

オリジナルのカイゼン・エクスプレス(上掲書、現在第２版)は、各国の日系工場で働く日本人と日本人以外の人々に活用してもらうことを意図してつくられました。英語はほとんどの多国籍企業の公用語ですから、日本人と日本人以外の人々が共にTPSを学ぶのに本書を使ってもらえたらうれしいと私たちは願っていました。そう、本書は、TPSの基本をカバーする入門書なのです。しかし、そうであればこそ、工場の人々がTPSを実践する最初の１、２年の間に学ぶ必要のある事項のほとんどを織り込みつつも、分かりやすいものであるべきです。

うれしいサプライズとしてやって来たのは、もっと「グローバルな」バージョンのカイゼン・エクスプレスをつくってほしいというリクエストでした。私たちがめざしたような、グローバルで分かりやすいTPSの入門書は、どの言語であれ、実のところまだ存在しないらしいのです。最初のリクエストは台湾からで、すぐれたTPS実践者であるJoe Lee(李兆華氏)と中衛発展中心が繁体字中国語の読者のためのカイゼン・エクスプレスを開発してくれました。

このたび、リーン・エンタープライズ・インスティテュートによって、他のさまざまな言語の対訳バージョンを容易に開発できるような形で再構成されたグローバル版をお届けできることを、私たちはとてもうれしく思います。私たちは、読者の皆さんが改善特急（カイゼン・エクスプレス）に乗って自身の改善の旅を続け、フィードバックを寄せてくれることを楽しみにしています。そして、私たちもまた、皆さんと同じように、私たちの改善の旅を続けるつもりです。

成沢　俊子　　　　ジョン・シュック
川崎　　　　　　　デトロイト

2009年３月

Introduction

"Kaizen" has transcended the Japanese language. A global term that no longer requires translation, it has come to mean many things to many people. With *Kaizen Express*, we express an approach to kaizen that is at once a return to basics while also emphasizing the centrality of experiential learning at the individual and team level. Many try to incorporate a kaizen mindset by focusing on theory, obscuring the fact that there are basic skills, routines, and tools that form the foundation for this approach. *Kaizen Express* is grounded in the belief that the thinking of the Toyota Production System (TPS) can only be achieved through doing: "It's easier to act your way to a new way of thinking than to think your way to a new way of acting."

Kaizen Express was originally developed as a set of bilingual TPS learning materials. The original scripts of *Kaizen Express* appeared serially in the Japanese magazine "Kojo Kanri" (*Factory Management*, Nikkan Kogyo Shinbun-sha) from 2005 to 2007 and subsequently compiled in the book *"Eigo de kaizen! Toyota Seisan Hoshiki—Kaizen Express"* (by the same publisher).

The original *Kaizen Express*, now in its second edition, was intended primarily as an aid to Japanese readers and to non-Japanese working at Japanese-affiliated factories around the globe. As English is the official language of most multinational companies, our hope was that Japanese and non-Japanese could use *Kaizen Express* to learn TPS together. So, *Kaizen Express* is a primer—covering the basics of TPS—but it is also comprehensive, covering most of the topics a production team might need to learn in its first year or two of implementing TPS.

It came as a pleasant surprise for us to receive requests for a more "global" version of *Kaizen Express*. Evidently, no similar global, comprehensive primer for TPS exists—in any language. The first request came from Taiwan, where TPS practitioner Joe Lee and Corporate Synergy Development Center have created a version of *Kaizen Express* for readers of traditional Chinese.

Now, we are pleased to offer this new global version of *Kaizen Express*, structured in a way that should make it easy to produce in multiple languages, through the Lean Enterprise Institute. We look forward to your feedback as you continue your own kaizen journey—we will continue ours as well, through *Kaizen Express*!

Toshiko Narusawa
Kawasaki
March 2009

John Shook
Detroit

Kaizen Express

CONTENTS

Chapter 1 初めて学ぶトヨタ生産方式 Let's Learn TPS

Chapter 2 ジャスト・イン・タイム Just-in-Time with Flow, Pull, and Heijunka

Chapter 3 自働化と設備改善 Jidoka and Machines

カイゼン・エクスプレス

CONTENTS

Chapter 4 工程の安定化 Process Stability

Chapter 5 改善に終わりなし The Lean Journey

改善フォーム集 Forms

Appendix-2 付録-2 プリント教材 Training Materials

ワードリスト＆索引 Word List & Index

Chapter

1

初めて学ぶトヨタ生産方式
Let's Learn TPS

初めて学ぶトヨタ生産方式 ― 1
Let's Learn TPS

ムダとは？

What Is Waste?

ムダをひとことで言うと？

ムダとは？
顧客にとっての価値を生み出さないのに、資源を消費しているもの、状態。

または

顧客が喜んで「お金を払いたい」とは思わないようなもの、状態。

Muda＝"Waste"

Muda?
Any activity that consumes resources without creating value for the customer.

or

Any activity for which the customer is not willing to pay.

7つのムダ

大野耐一氏は、現場のムダを７つに分類しました。

Seven Wastes

Taiichi Ohno's categorization of the seven major wastes typically found at any gemba (workplace):

①つくりすぎのムダ

顧客や後工程が要求している量・タイミング・速度よりも、多く、早く、速く、つくってしまうこと。

Overproduction

Producing more, sooner, or faster than is required by the next process or customer.

②手待ちのムダ

作業者が何もせずに何かを待っていること。マシンサイクル待ちや設備の復旧待ち、部品の遅れ待ちなど。

Waiting

Operators standing idle as machines cycle, equipment fails, parts delay, etc.

動作のムダの見方

Categories of Work Motion Diagram

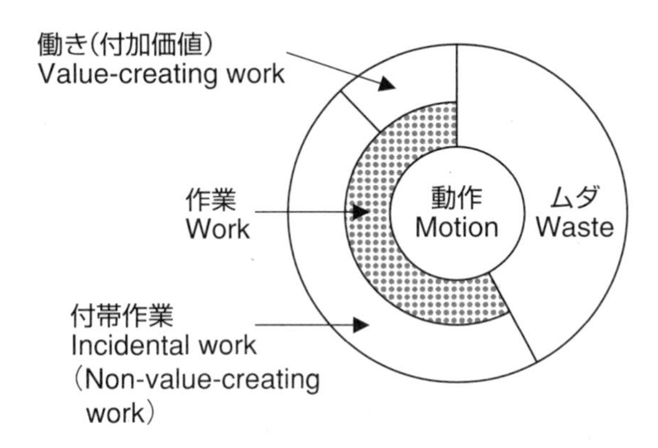

③運搬のムダ……**Conveyance**

運搬はそれ自体がムダ。なぜなら、付加価値をまったく生まないから。もちろん、部品や製品は運ばざるを得ませんが、運搬のムダは最小限にしなくてはいけません。

Conveyance itself is waste because it creates no value. Obviously parts and products must be transported, but any movement beyond the absolute minimum is muda.

④加工そのもののムダ……**Processing (or overprocessing)**

必要のない加工、正しくない加工。

Unnecessary or incorrect processing.

⑤在庫のムダ……**Inventory**

余分な材料、部品、仕掛品、完成品を持つこと。さらに正確に言えば、きちっと運用されている後工程引取り方式において、決められた量よりも、多く持つこと。

Keeping unnecessary raw materials, parts, WIP (work-in-process), and finished goods. More precisely, keeping more than the minimum stock necessary for a well-controlled pull system.

⑥動作のムダ……**Motion**

作業者の動作のうち、付加価値を生まないもの。作業者のみならず、機械の動きの中にも、動作のムダを見つけることができる。

Operators making movements that are creating no value. We can also identify waste in the motion of machines.

⑦不良をつくるムダ……**Correction**

検査、手直し、不良の廃棄。

Inspection, rework, and scrap.

停滞のムダと、動作・運搬のムダ
Accumulation / Movement & Conveyance

ムダの発見と廃除には、次の2つのムダの分類がとても役立ちます。
Try looking for it from these viewpoints:

❶ Accumulation

モノに着目した、**停滞のムダ**
See stops, delays, or accumulation by focusing on the flow of the product.

❷ Movement & Conveyance

動きに着目した、**動作・運搬のムダ**
See non-value-creating motion by focusing on the movement of people and machines.

ワンポイントレッスン ❶ One-Point Advice ❶

ムラ、ムリ、ムダを語りたい Mura, Muri, and Muda

ムダは、ムラとムリと深く絡んでいます。ムラは "fluctuation"（ばらつき、ゆらぎ、安定していないこと）、ムリは "overburden"（過負荷や残業）。

Muda is deeply intertwined with mura and muri. Mura means fluctuation and muri means overburden.

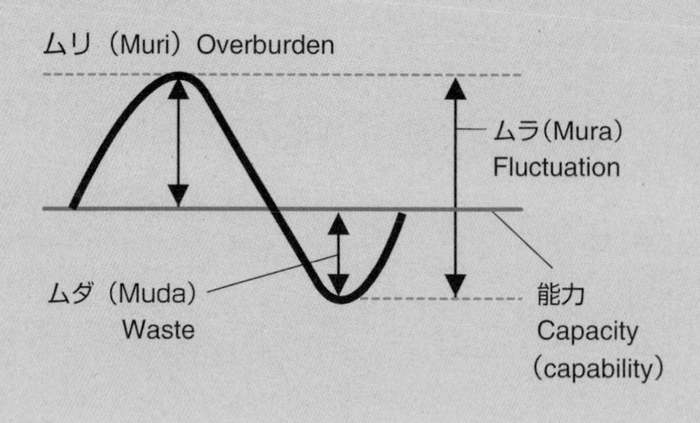

ワンポイントレッスン ② One-Point Advice ②

カタカナのムダ ひらがなのむだ 漢字の無駄

Three levels of *muda* differentiated by "katakana," "hiragana," or "kanji"

７つのムダとは別に、トヨタ生産方式では、カタカナのムダ、ひらがなのむだ、漢字の無駄、を使い分けます。

In addition to the seven types of wastes, there are three "levels" of waste that are differentiated in Japanese by writing "muda" in each of the three Japanese writing systems: *katakana* ("ムダ"), *hiragana* ("むだ"), or *kanji* ("無駄").

カタカナのムダは、点の改善ですぐに取れるムダ、という意味で使います。

- Muda in katakana ("ムダ") refers to waste that can be eliminated quickly by point kaizen.

ひらがなのむだは、すぐは取れないむだ、という意味で使います。より広い意味でのシステムレベルに潜む真因を取り除くためには、きちんとした取り組みが必要です。

- Muda in hiragana ("むだ") refers to waste that cannot be eliminated immediately; it must be tackled at its source at a broader system level.

漢字の無駄は、ある種の経営方針によって引き起こされている無駄、という意味で使います。たとえば、最終的には売れるだろうという希望的観測に基づいてたくさんの完成品在庫を持っているような場合です。

- Muda in kanji ("無駄") refers to waste that is a result of specific management policies, such as holding large amounts of finished goods hoping that they might eventually be sold.

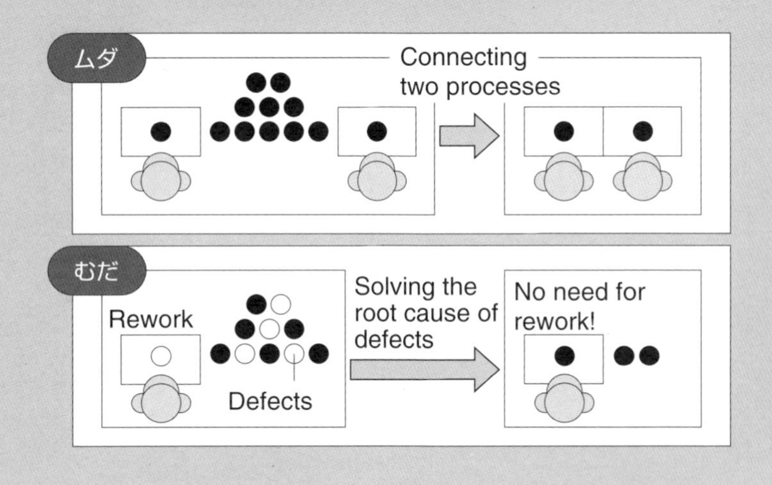

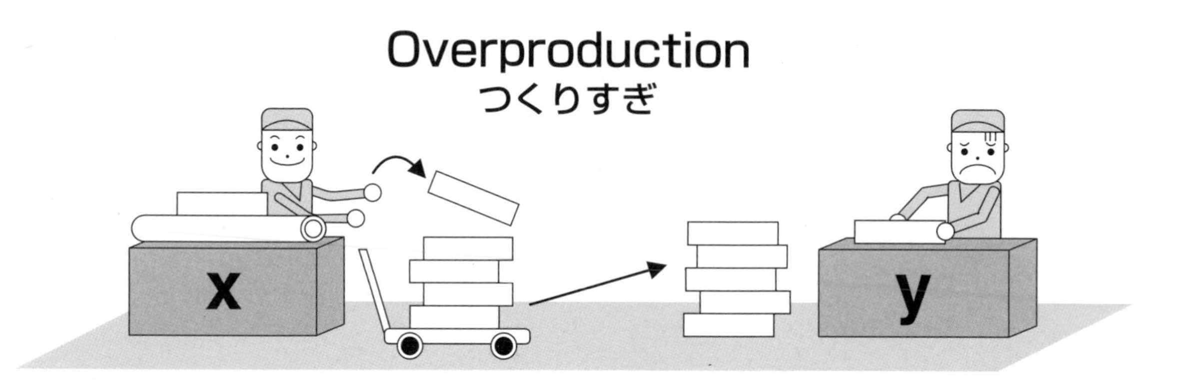

Let's talk

つくりすぎに気付こう！
Learn to see overproduction!

A: つくりすぎは最も悪いムダです。

A: Overproduction is the worst form of waste.

B: どうして？

B: Why?

A: つくりすぎは、その他のいろいろなムダのもととなり、ムダを見えなくしてしまうから。たとえば、在庫や不良、余計な運搬。

A: Because it generates and hides other wastes, such as inventory, defects, and excess transport.

B: ということは、私たちの現場にもつくりすぎのムダがある？

B: So, do you think we have overproduction at our workplace?

A: その通り。工程xと工程yの間に、仕掛りがあるでしょう？　これがつくりすぎです。いくつありますか？

A: Without question! There is some WIP between process x and process y. That is the waste of overproduction. How many pieces are there?

B: 10個です。どうすればよいですか？

B: Ten pieces. How do we eliminate them?

A: xとyの間を詰める。そして、仕掛りを１つに保つのです。どうですか？

A: Let's connect the two processes, then keep just one piece between x and y. What do you think about that kaizen?

B: yの作業が終わるまでxが手待ちになります。

B: But, then operator x will have to wait on operator y to finish his work.

A: タクトタイムは何秒？　タクトタイムに合わせて１人で作業するか、または作業を再配分してはどうですか？

A: Okay. What is the takt time? How about trying to match the takt time with one operator or by redistributing the work elements?

初めて学ぶトヨタ生産方式 — 2
Let's Learn TPS

トヨタ生産方式とは？
What Is TPS?

トヨタ生産方式とは？

トヨタ生産方式(TPS)とは、企業の競争力を高めるための理念と手法のフレームワークです。

What Is TPS?

The Toyota Production System (TPS) is a framework of concepts and methods to enhance corporate vitality.

トヨタ生産方式が目指すもの

トヨタ生産方式とは、徹底したムダ廃除を通してより良い品質、より低いコスト、より短いリードタイムを実現するために、トヨタ自動車で創案され、工夫されてきた生産方式です。

トヨタ生産方式は考え方であるとともに、トヨタの先人の努力の結集としての手法体系でもあります。したがって、過去から今日に至るまでの手法体系をして「TPSとは」と語ることは困難です。TPSには、これで完成という形はないからです。しかしながら、TPSを簡潔に語る必要があるときは、次のような説明が役立つでしょう。

The Goal of TPS

TPS is the production system developed by the Toyota Motor Corporation to provide the best quality, the lowest cost, and the shortest lead time through the elimination of waste.

TPS is a way of thinking and the framework of methods accomplished through the efforts of many Toyota people over the course of many years. It is impossible to define TPS by only looking at its past-and-present methodologies, as there is no perfect condition in TPS. Hopefully, however, the following explanations will help.

トヨタ生産方式の２本柱

トヨタ生産方式の２本柱は、にんべんのついた自働化とジャスト・イン・タイムです。そのイメージは、次ページの図のような「家」の形で表現されます。

Two Pillars of TPS

The two pillars of TPS are “jidoka” and “just-in-time.” The basic image of TPS is often illustrated with the “house” shown here.

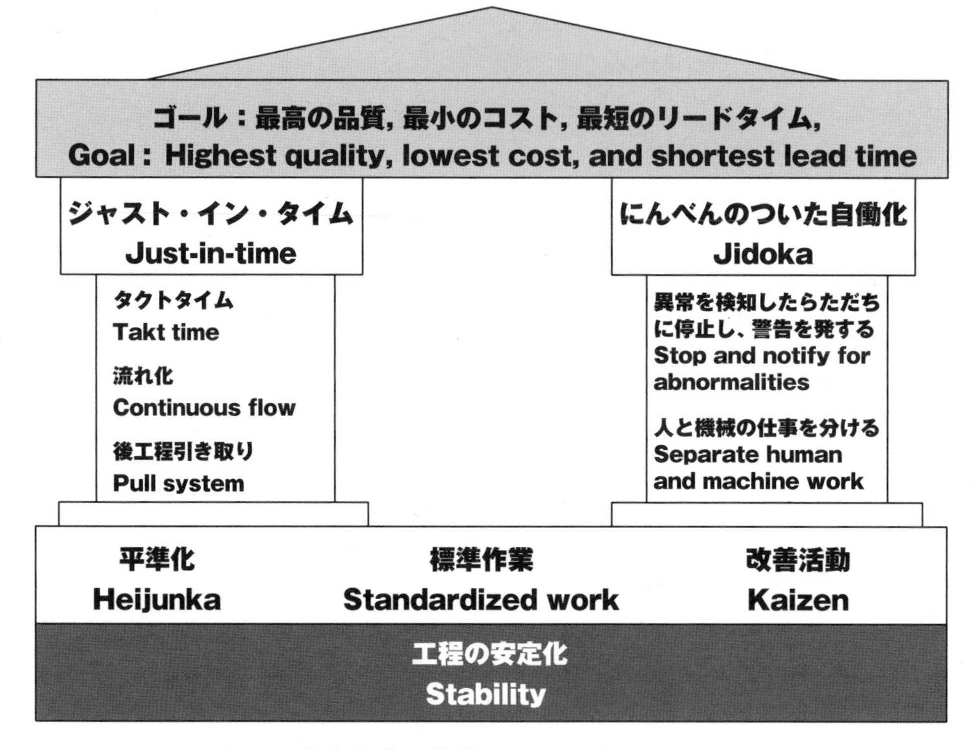

トヨタ生産方式の基本のイメージ：TPSハウス
Basic Image of the Toyota Production System: the TPS House

トヨタ生産方式の誕生と大野耐一氏

Taiichi Ohno and the Birth of TPS

豊田喜一郎氏が国産乗用車の開発を目指してトヨタ自動車工業（自工）を設立したのは1937年のことです。6年後、豊田紡織の自工への合併に伴い大野耐一氏（1912−1990）が自工へ転籍。戦後、喜一郎氏は「3年でアメリカに追いつけ！」という高い目標を掲げて会社の再生を率いました。

Kiichiro Toyoda founded the Toyota Motor Company (TMC) in 1937. Taiichi Ohno (1912-1990) moved to TMC from the Toyoda Boshoku Company six years later. After WWII, Kiichiro set the foundation for the TMC's remarkable later growth by declaring an aggressive target: "Catch up with the productivity of the U.S. within three years!"

トヨタ生産方式が生まれたのは第二次世界大戦後の1947年のことでした。大野耐一氏がトヨタの機械工場で「手待ちのムダ」を発見したのです。

TPS was essentially born in 1947 in the post-WWII period when Taiichi Ohno analyzed Toyota's machining shop and identified the waste of waiting.

大野氏は後にトヨタ自動車工業の副社長となりますが、トヨタ生産方式が今日見るような統合的なシステムとして築かれていく過程で、最も大きく貢献した人物です。

Ohno—who later became an executive vice president at Toyota—was the man who did the most to structure TPS as an integrated framework.

ワンポイントレッスン One-Point Advice

二人の偉人とTPSの２本柱

にんべんのついた自働化とジャスト・イン・タイムのルーツはともに戦前（第二次世界大戦前）にあります。自働化は豊田佐吉翁が大正年間に発明した自動織機にその源があります。ジャスト・イン・タイムは、佐吉翁の子息・豊田喜一郎氏が自動車をできるだけムダなくつくりたいと考え、会社の方針として1938年に提唱したものです。

Two Great Creators and the Roots of the Two Pillars of TPS

Jidoka and just-in-time both have their roots in the prewar (pre-WWII) period. Jidoka originated in the automatic loom developed by Sakichi Toyoda in the Taisho Period (1912–1926). Just-in-time was declared company policy by Kiichiro Toyoda in 1938 with the aim of producing cars with as little waste as possible.

佐吉翁とにんべんのついた自働化

佐吉翁の自動織機は、**縦糸が切れたら即座に止まります**。これによって品質は劇的に改善され、作業者は機械の見張り番から開放されて多台持ちが可能になりました。
異常を検知したら即座に停止し警告を発するように機械を設計するというこの考え方は、後にトヨタで「にんべんのついた自働化」と呼ばれ、**トヨタのあらゆる設備、あらゆる生産ライン、あらゆる仕事のやり方にとって不可欠なものになりました**。（3章参照）

Jidoka and Sakichi Toyoda

Sakichi' s automatic looms would **stop immediately whenever a warp thread broke.** Doing so dramatically improved quality and freed operators from just monitoring machines, making it possible for an operator to handle multiple machines.
The concept of designing machines to stop automatically and call immediate attention to problems came to be called “jidoka,” or later “automation with a human touch” and became **a critical feature of every machine, every production line, and every Toyota operation.** (See Chapter 3.)

喜一郎氏とジャスト・イン・タイム

喜一郎氏は1938年にジャスト・イン・タイムの概念を提唱しました。喜一郎氏はまたフォード・システムを深く研究し、日本の事情に合わせて適用しようとしていました。

Kiichiro Toyoda and Just-in-Time

Kiichiro proposed the concept of “just-in-time” in 1938. He had also studied Fordism and tried to adopt and adapt it to fit to the conditions of Japanese companies.

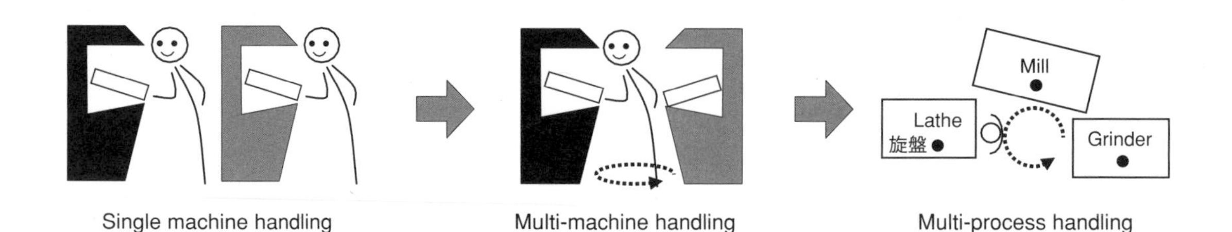

Single machine handling
1台持ち（単能工）

Multi-machine handling
多台持ち（単能工）

Multi-process handling
多工程持ち（多能工）

Let's talk 自働化と多台持ち、多工程持ち
Jidoka enables multi-machine and multi-process handling!

A: 大野さんが初めて手待ちのムダを発見したとき、多台持ちにしたと聞くけれど、大野さんはどうやって多台持ちを思いついたの？

A: I have heard that Mr. Ohno tried multi-machine handling when he identified the waste of waiting for the first time. How did he get that idea?

B: 大野さんは豊田紡織での経験から、自働化の機構があれば、1人の作業者が何十台もの織機を持てることを知っていたんだ。

B: From his experience at Toyoda Boshoku, he had known that a jidoka device had enabled a single operator to handle dozens of looms.

A: だから、機械の見張りはムダだと気づくことができたのね！　次に、大野さんが気づいたのがつくりすぎのムダですね。どうしてつくりすぎがムダだと気づくことができたのかしら？

A: So he could find the waste of monitoring machines! Next, Mr. Ohno found the waste of overproduction. Why was he able to identify it as waste?

B: 戦後、大野さんはできるだけ早くアメリカの生産性に追いつき、追い抜きたいという目標を持っていた。国内市場は小さく、戦争で傷ついた日本経済にはお金もなかった。だから、アメリカの大量生産とは違う方法を見つけるしかなかったんだよ。

B: In the post-WWII period, Mr. Ohno had the objective to outstrip the productivity in the U.S. as soon as possible. The domestic market was small and the war-torn Japanese economy was starved for capital. So Toyota had to find some new way that was different from mass production in the U.S.

A: とうとう、大野さんはロットを小さくして、段取り替えを速やかにすることでつくりすぎを抑え、結果として安くつくることができると証明したのですね。

A: Eventually, Mr. Ohno proved that producing smaller batches with quick changeovers actually resulted in cost savings while preventing overproduction.

初めて学ぶトヨタ生産方式 — 3
Let's Learn TPS

TPSが人と設備に求めるもの

TPS Puts People and Machines Together!

人も設備も変わらなければ！

なめらかな流れを実現するには、顧客の要求に合わせて、一人ひとりの従業員、すべてのマネージャー、すべてのサプライヤー、そして設備も、変わらなければなりません。

TPS Means Change!

Creating a smooth stream requires that every employee, every manager, every supplier, and every machine will change, to meet the requirements of the customers.

TPSの「能率」は、従来の考え方とはぜんぜん違う！

① 見かけの能率と真の能率
② 個々の能率と全体の効率

TPS Looks at "Efficiency" in Radically Different Ways Compared with Conventional Thinking!

① Apparent efficiency vs. true efficiency
② Local efficiency vs. total productivity

①見かけの能率と真の能率

見かけの能率

売れ行きに関係なく、現状の人や設備のまま生産量を増やすこと。これは、単なる計算上の能率向上に過ぎない。

① Apparent efficiency vs. true efficiency

Apparent efficiency

Apparent efficiency means increasing production output with no change in the number of operators or equipment, without being tied to sales or market demands. It is an improvement mathematically only.

真の能率 ……………………………… **True efficiency**

売れる数量だけを、最少限の人と設備で生産し、能率を上げる方法。限量経営の考え方からきており、真の原価低減に結びつく。

True efficiency means producing the number of parts or products that can be sold while utilizing the minimum number of operators and equipment possible. True efficiency is the result of "Genryo Management" and results in true cost reduction.

②個々の能率と全体の効率

② Local efficiency vs. total productivity

また大野氏は、個々の能率だけを追求し過ぎるとつくりすぎを生み、全体の効率を損なう場合があることに注意しなくてはならない、と言っています。

As Taiichi Ohno pointed out, we have to be aware that pursuing only local efficiency will cause overproduction and sometimes diminish total productivity.

個々の能率 ……………………………… **Local efficiency**

前後の工程やお客様とは無関係に、個々の工程の能率を追求すること。

Local efficiency means boosting the efficiency at a certain line, process, or machine, completely separated from previous or following processes or customers.

全体の効率 ……………………………… **Total productivity**

個々の工程における見かけの能率ではなく、流れの全域にわたって真の能率を向上させて、企業全体の生産性を高めること。

Rather than pursuing apparent efficiency at one local point, total productivity means seeking to improve true efficiency through the entire production flow, which results in greater overall company productivity. (Sometimes called "system efficiency")

多能工化と設備改善で流れ化を

People and Machines Contribute to Realize Continuous Flows!

多能工化 ……………………………… **Multi-skilled operator**

流れをつくり、真の能率を向上させるためには、作業者は、いろいろな機械の操作や、多種の作業を担当できなくてはなりません。

To create continuous flow and improve true efficiency, an operator must be able to perform many different jobs and operate diverse types of machines.

設備改善 ……………………………… **Right-sized equipment**

流れの中で設備を活かすには、タクトタイムに合った速度で正しく動作し、大き過ぎず、かつ安価という新しいタイプの設備が必要です。これを、私たちは **"right-sized"** と呼んでいます。

To place equipment in the production flow, we need equipment that runs at the rate to match takt time, is less expensive, and is not too large. We call this "right-sized" equipment.

ワンポイントレッスン One-Point Advice

リーンな設備とリーンな人をつくりだすためのキーポイント
Key Points for Developing Lean Equipment and People

(1)リーンな設備をつくるためのキーポイント　Key points for equipment

設備改善の着眼点 …… **"Right-sized"tools and equipment**

①付加価値を生む部分に注目する …… **① Focus on the actual value-creating part**

機械の中の、付加価値を生まないムダな動きや搬送をできるだけ小さくします。

Motion and conveyance in the machine that does not create value should be minimized.

②必要な能力(不良ゼロ、タクトタイム) …… **② Capability to meet customer requirements**

不良をつくらず、想定されるタクトタイムで動くことが求められますが、タクトタイム以上に速く動く必要はありません。

Equipment must be capable to run at the rate of estimated takt time while making no defects. But it does not need to run more quickly than takt time.

③メンテナンスしやすい …… **③ Easy to maintain**

④可動率を高く …… **④ High operational availability**

動くべきときには正しく動かなくてはなりません。

It must be available whenever needed to run.

⑤素早い段取り替えが可能 …… **⑤ Easy to changeover quickly**

⑥移設が簡単 …… **⑥ Easy to move**

⑦より小さく、より安く …… **⑦ Smaller and lower cost**

(2)リーンな人をつくるためのキーポイント　Key points for people

管理者は、作業者に対する教育訓練プログラムを日常的に実施する必要があります。スキル管理板は、訓練計画の基本をなすものです。

Managers should always provide training for operators. The Skills Training Matrix Board is the basis of the training plan.

Skills Training Matrix

◔ Can do generally　◕ Certified　◑ Can do well　● Can do training

Factory name:	Foreman:
Made By:	Date:

#	Operator	Cut	Bend	Grind	Weld	Test	Repair	Assem	M.Test	E.Test	Shipping	Current Date	Target Date
1	Operator A	●	●	●	◕	◕	◑	○	◔	○	○		
2	Operator B	◕	◕	◑	◑	◔	◔	○	○	○	○		
3	Operator C	○	○	○	○	○	○	●	●	●	●		
	…												

(Processes: Cut through Shipping)

人の心を変えるのは設備よりも難しい

Changing People is Harder Than Changing Equipment!

改善の成果を分かち合おう！

Improvement Leads to Shared Success

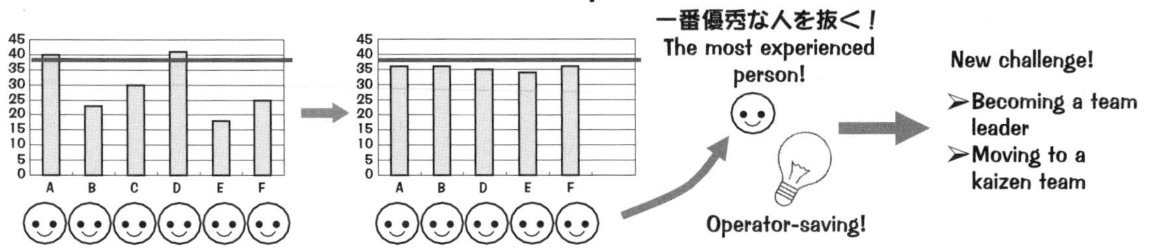

Let's talk 改善の成果を分かち合う Explain the benefits of kaizen!

A: 今までの改善で、ラインから作業者を抜くことができました。でも、その結果が失業だとしたら、これ以上は、誰だって協力しようとは思えないですよね？

A: We have freed up some operators through kaizen. But surely nobody will be willing to support kaizen if it results in loss of employment.

B: よい指摘です。どのような仕事であれ、永遠に変わらぬままということはあり得ませんが、可能な限り雇用を守るのは経営の責務です。

B: Good point! While no task stays the same forever, management should try to provide secure employment as long as possible.

A: そうあってほしいわ。雇用を脅かされる心配がないのなら、誰でもアイデアを出したり、それを実現したりしたいと、強く願っているはずよ。

A: We all hope so. I think that people are usually eager to give and realize their ideas for more kaizen if it doesn't threaten job security.

B: そうだね。抜いた作業者について、きちんとした計画をマネジメントは持つべきです。別の意義ある仕事についてもらわなくては。

B: I think so, too. Therefore, management needs to have a reliable plan for them once they are freed from their current work. They need to go to other meaningful work.

A: チームリーダーになる訓練はどうかしら。

A: How about training to become a team leader?

B: その通り。だから、ラインから人を抜くときは、ナンバーワンの熟練者を選んで、その人に新たな挑戦をしてもらう。リーダーになるとか、推進室に移ってもらうとか。

B: Yes. So, when you get one operator-saving, you take the most experienced operator and set him or her to new challenges, such as being a leader, or moving to the Lean Promotion Team.

A: それなら、改善の目的が、単に人数を減らすことではなくて、現場をよりよくすることや、人の能力を引き出すことにあるんだ、ということが私たちにもよくわかるわ。

A: That is a nice way for us to recognize that the purpose of kaizen is to make processes better and to develop people's abilities, not to simply reduce the number of operators.

Chapter

2

ジャスト・イン・タイム
Just-in-Time with Flow, Pull, and Heijunka

ジャスト・イン・タイム — 1
Just-in-Time with Flow, Pull, and Heijunka

ジャスト・イン・タイム
What Is Just-in-Time?

ジャスト・イン・タイムとは？

ジャスト・イン・タイムとは、必要なものを、必要なときに、必要なだけつくり、提供する生産システムのことです。

What Is Just-in-Time?

Just-in-time means a system of production that makes and delivers what is needed, just when it is needed, and just in the amount needed.

ジャスト・イン・タイムが目指すもの

それでは、「必要」とはどんな意味なのでしょうか。トヨタ生産方式では、お客様を起点に考えます。

お客様は、より良い製品を、より安く、できるだけ早く欲しいと考えます。

そして、お客様の満足と生産サイドの効率化をともに達成しようとするのです。

ジャスト・イン・タイムは、徹底したムダ廃除を通して、より良い品質のものを、より低いコスト、より少ない資源、より短いリードタイムで製造し、お客様に提供することを目指したものです。

Why Just-in-Time?

What does the word “needed” mean? How do we know how much is needed? Start with the customer!

Customers want the best possible products at the lowest possible prices. And they want them as soon as possible.

Pursue both customer satisfaction *and* your internal efficiencies!

Just-in-time aims for the total elimination of all waste to achieve the best possible quality, the lowest possible cost and use of resources, and the shortest possible production and delivery lead times.

Just-In-Time Relies on Heijunka and Is Comprised of Three Elements

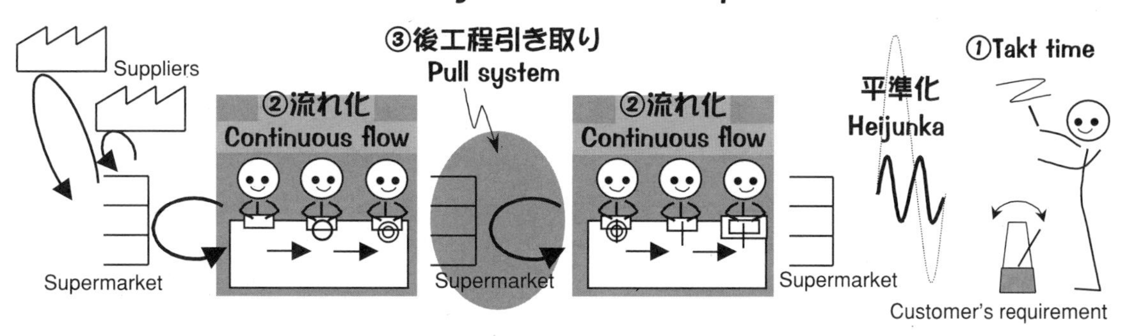

ジャスト・イン・タイムの３つの要素

ジャスト・イン・タイムは平準化を大前提とし、3つの要素で支えられます。タクトタイム、流れ化、後工程引き取りです。

The Three Elements of Just-in-Time

Just-in-time relies on heijunka as a foundation and is comprised of three elements: takt time, continuous flow, and a pull system.

タクトタイムと流れ化、後工程引き取り

Takt Time, Continous Flow, and Pull

タクトタイムと流れ化、後工程引き取りは、ジャスト・イン・タイムを支える要素ですが、この3つは、密接につながり合って初めて成果として結実するものです。

These three elements support just-in-time well only when they are properly integrated.

タクトタイムとは、お客様の要求に合うように、売れに合わせて、部品1個、製品1個をどのくらいの速さでつくればよいかを示すものです。

Takt time is how often you should produce one part or product to meet customer requirements based on the rate of sales.

流れ化とは、タクトタイムに合わせて、1度に1個ずつ、1つの工程から次の工程へと停滞なく(ほかのいろいろなムダもなく)、すいすいと流れていく1個流しを意味します。

Continuous flow means producing and moving one item at a time to match takt time, with each item passed immediately from one process step to the next without stagnation (or any other waste) in between.

トヨタ生産方式の中核をなす考え方は、売れに合わせて、すべての工程を加工の順番に並べて1本のスムーズな流れをつくること、です。

A core concept of TPS is arranging all the processes in the production sequence in a single, smooth flow based on the rate of sales.

しかし、すべての工程を1個流しでつなぐことは、最初はなかなか難しいものです。上流工程へ目を向けると、クリーンルーム内でなければ加工できない、高額な高速設備で加工している、また、ほかの製品群との共用で専用化は不可能、というようなケースが多いものです。これらすべてをはじめから1個流しでつなぐことは、現実的とは言えません。

In initial stages, it may sometimes be difficult to connect all your processes in a continuous flow. Especially in upstream processes, there are various cases where immediately implementing a continuous flow is hard: clean-rooms may be necessary, expensive machines are required for some processes, or some machines must be shared. Those cases present challenges and opportunities to integrate the three elements more completely.

最初は、流れ化と後工程引き取りの組合せから始めるのがよいでしょう。そして、工程の安定化や段取り改善、インライン設備の開発などに合わせて、流れ化の範囲を広げていくのです。

A good approach can be to begin with a combination of continuous flow and pull system. Then extend the range of continuous flow as reliability is improved, changeover times are reduced, and in-line equipment is developed.

ワンポイントレッスン One-Point Advice

タクトタイムを計算する

Calculation of Takt Time

タクトタイム

$$= \frac{\text{シフト当たりの定時稼働時間}}{\text{シフト当たりの要求数量}}$$

例：27,000秒÷455個＝59秒/個

Takt Time

$$= \frac{\text{Available working time per shift}}{\text{Customer demand rate per shift}}$$

Example: 27,000 sec.÷455 pieces＝59 sec./piece

タクトタイムに合わせてつくることは単純と感じられるかもしれませんが、努力なしには成り立ちません。

- 問題に対して素早く（タクト内で）対応する
- 想定外のダウンの原因をなくす
- 段取り時間を短縮する

Producing to takt time sounds simple, but is the result of concentrated efforts to:

- provide fast response (within takt time) to problems
- eliminate causes of unplanned downtime
- reduce changeover time

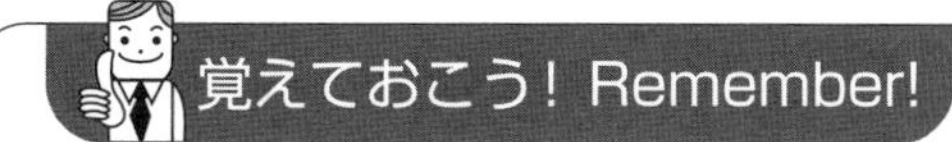

米国で再発見されたモノと情報の流れ図

点の改善（個々の工程の作業改善や設備改善）は重要です。しかし、ムダの真因を見つけ、全体を改善するためには（＝線の改善）、工場全体、さらには顧客から商品物流、サプライヤーまでも含めた全体を視野に入れて、改善計画を立てることが欠かせません。

そこで、このような「システム改善」に役立つのが、バリュー・ストリーム・マッピング（VSM）です。しかし、おもしろいことにVSMはあまり日本では知られておらず、単に「モノと情報の流れの図」と呼ばれていました。

点の改善は不可欠ですが、ムダの真因を見つけて、全体を改善する実行計画を立案し、実現するためには、VSMがとても役立ちます。設計図なしに家を建てることを想像してみてください。

Value-Stream Mapping Popularized in the U.S.

Point kaizen (motion improvement and machine improvement at each process) itself is important. However, achieving greater system-level efficiency requires a system-level view. And performing “system kaizen” requires seeing the entire extended value stream in order to improve performance from end to end—the entire plant, customers, logistics, and suppliers.
For system kaizen, value-stream mapping (VSM) is very helpful. Interestingly, VSM was not so well-known in Japan, where it was called “Material and Information Flow Mapping.”

Process kaizen is critical. However, VSM is useful to identify the sources of waste and to plan and realize total system kaizen. Imagine trying to build a house without a blueprint!

Future-State Map（将来）

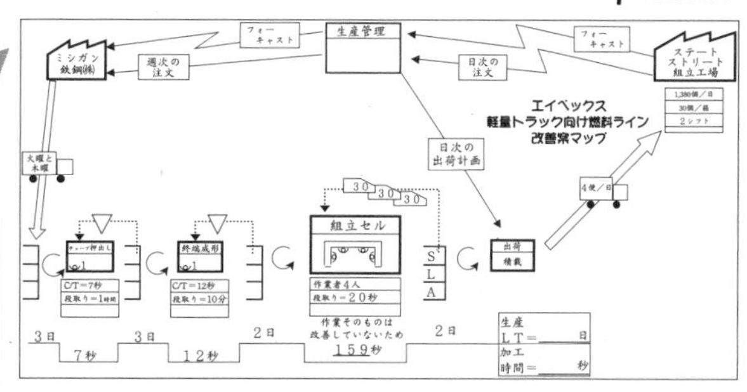

Current-State Map（現状）

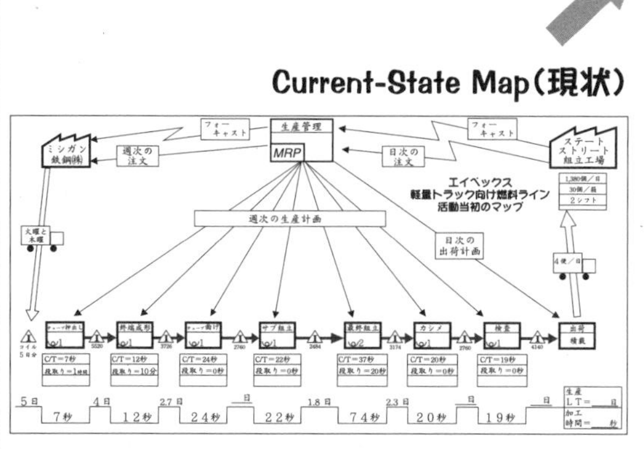

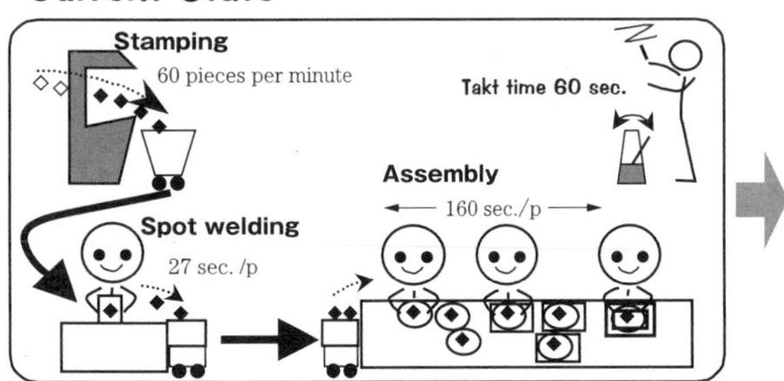

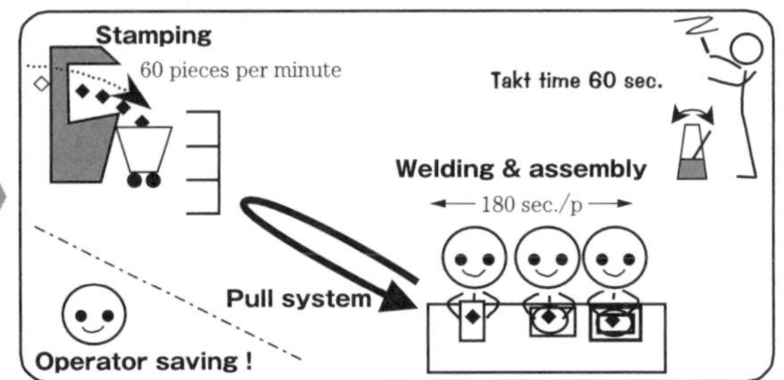

Let's talk 流れ化で直接つなぐvs.引き取りでつなぐ
Choose the best way in each case: create continuous flow or connect with a pull system?

A: ここが私たちの現場です。最初の工程はプレス、次がスポット溶接、最後が組立です。

A: Here is our workplace. The first process is stamping, then spot-welding, and the final process is assembly.

B: タクトタイムは何秒ですか？　それから、各工程では、何秒かかっていますか？

B: What is your takt time? And, how many seconds does it take for each process?

A: タクトタイムは60秒。組立は全部で160秒、溶接は27秒です。プレスは自動加工で、1分間に60個。プレスはこの製品だけの専用ではありません。

A: Takt time is 60 seconds. Total work time is 160 seconds per piece at assembly, and 27 seconds at welding. Stamping automatically produces 60 pieces per minute. Stamping is not dedicated for this product.

B: 溶接と組立で187秒、187秒をタクトタイム60で割ると3.12。まずは、溶接から組立までを流れ化し、4人ではなく、3人編成とするべきです。

B: Total work time is 187 seconds for welding and assembly. Then we get 3.12 by dividing 187 seconds by takt time 60. So we should first connect welding to assembly as a continuous flow and assign three operators, not four.

A: すごいわ！　1人抜くことができますね！　プレスはどうしましょう？

A: Great! We can get one operator-saving! What should we do about stamping?

B: 今すぐにプレスを流れ化するのは、現実的ではありません。プレスのサイクルは高速過ぎるし、ほかの製品のために段取り替えも必要です。ですから、プレス設備を改善するまでの間は、後工程引き取りを採用しなければなりません。

B: Incorporating stamping into a continuous flow right now is not practical. Its cycle is too quick for this product and it changes over for other products. So we should use a pull system until the stamping machine will be right-sized.

ジャスト・イン・タイム — 2
Just-in-Time with Flow, Pull, and Heijunka

流れ化
What Is Continuous Flow?

流れ化とは？

流れ化とは、タクトタイムに合わせて、可能な限り工程順につないだ1本の流れに沿って、1度に1つずつ（あるいは小さな一定量ずつ）、つくり、運ぶことです。各工程では、次の工程が求める分だけをつくります。

1個流しの流れ化を“Continuous Flow”と呼び、一般的な流れについて言及するときは単に“Flow”と呼んで、使い分けることによって、改善への理解が深まるはずです。

What Is Continuous Flow?

Continuous flow means producing and moving one item at a time (or a small and consistent batch) through a series of processing steps as continuously as possible, to match takt time, with each step making just what is required by the next step.

You may find it effective to use a different term for the specific method of creating single-piece flow, or “continuous flow,” and more generally speaking, “flow.”

フォード式生産と流れ

流れ生産は、ヘンリー・フォード氏（1863—1947）が米国ミシガン州ハイランドパークで実現した革新的な生産システムにそのルーツがあります。フォードは、1台の車をつくるのにかかる時間とコストを、着実かつ劇的に削減しました。組立のリードタイムは12時間以上から1時間半に、車の価格は780ドルから360ドルになったのです。フォードの流れ生産は、今日に至る工業社会に計り知れないインパクトを与えました。

Fordism and Flow

Flow production was a revolutionary system originated by Henry Ford (1863–1947) at Highland Park, Michigan. Through continuing innovations, Ford steadily and dramatically reduced the time and cost of producing a car. Assembly lead time was reduced from over 12 hours to about an hour and a half, cutting the price of an automobile from $780 to $360. Ford's flow production had a tremendous impact on modern industrial societies.

フォード式流れ生産における技術革新 ………………… **The innovations of the Ford system**

- 部品に一定の互換性を持たせ、ライン上の各作業のサイクルタイムのばらつきをなくす。
- 組立のライン化それ自体が革新的で画期的。
- 部品の加工方法を見直し、機械を加工順に並べて、機械から機械へ、素早く滑らかに流す。
- 最終組立ラインの部品所要に合わせて部品を加工するように、生産管理システムを整備する。

- Consistently interchangeable parts so that cycle times could be stable for every job along an extended line.
- The assembly line itself.
- The reconfiguration of parts fabrication tasks so that machines were lined up in process sequence with parts flowing quickly and smoothly from machine to machine.
- A production control system ensuring that the rate of parts fabrication matched the consumption rate of parts in final assembly.

フォード式とトヨタ生産方式 Fordism and TPS

トヨタは、フォード式から多くを学んでTPSの骨格をつくりました。TPSの理想の一つは、ムービング・組立ラインの流れを可能な限り拡張することです。「流れ化」ラインは、フォードのムービング・ラインの考え方を継ぐ、進化した後継者と言えるでしょう。まだ小さかった日本市場に合うように、工夫されてきたものです。

Toyota included much from Fordism in the structure of TPS. An ideal of TPS is to extend the flow of the moving assembly line as far as possible. "Continuous flow" cells could be regarded as an evolutionary successor of the moving-line concept of Ford. To meet the Japanese small market in those days, it had been developed.

1950年代のトヨタは、小さなロットで、より安く、より速く、車をつくる方法を開発するほかなかったのです。

Toyota in the 1950s had to develop some new methods to produce cars more quickly in smaller lots at lower cost.

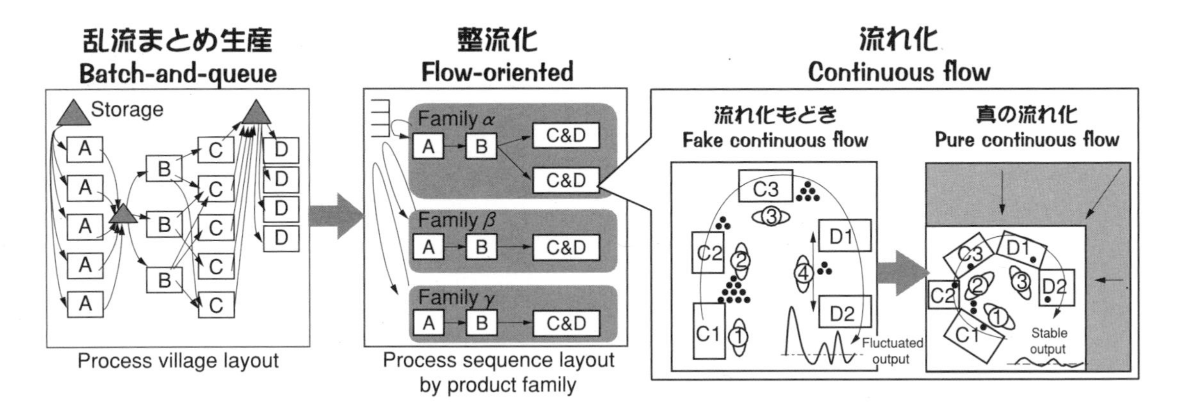

単なる「流れ」から、流れ化へ

From Flow to Pure Continuous Flow

素材から製品を完成するまで、**最も速い方法**は流れ化なのに、歴史的に、私たちは大量生産の考え方に基づいて、**分業型レイアウト**を採ってきました。人間は、直感的に、まとめることを好むのかもしれません。

Even though the **fastest way** to translate raw material into finished products is continuous flow, historically we have adopted **process village layouts** based on the concept of mass production. The human mind may like batches intuitively!

流れ化実現へのステップ

The road to continuous flow

①製品ごとの工程経路を分析し**製品群を定義する。**

① **Defining the product families** through analyzing paths for each item.

②**可能な限り、すべての工程を**加工順に並べる。

② Relocating process steps, **wherever possible**, into process sequences for product families.

③もう一度、**「流れ化の目で」**見て改善する。
- タクトタイムと出来高のバラツキ
- 工程間の仕掛品の停滞
- 動作のムダ

③ Looking again at the flow with **"eyes for continuous flow"** to realize pure continuous flow.
- –Fluctuated output in discord with takt time
- –Small stagnation between steps
- –Waste of motion

ワンポイントトレッスン One-Point Advice

流れ化の着眼点

A Closer Look with Eyes for Continuous Flow

①出来高のバラツキ
まず、**生産管理板**を見る（なければあなたがつくること）。どのような理由であれ、タクトタイムに対する出来高のばらつきは、大きな改善可能性の存在を示す。

① Fluctuating output
First, look at the Production Analysis Board. (If there is no Board, make one yourself!) Whatever the cause, fluctuating output that is slower or quicker than takt time is clear evidence that line performance can be greatly improved.

②工程間の停滞
工程間に停滞があるのなら、そこには必ず問題がある。真因を突き止めなくてはならない。

② Stagnation between steps
Wherever there is stagnation between steps, there are problems. You have to find the root cause.

③人の動き
繰返しのサイクルから外れた動きはバッチ作業の可能性大。手待ちは**分業**によって生じる場合が多い。動作のムダは**部品の置き方**の悪さを示す。

③ Operator's motion
Operators leaving their regular work often means they are working in batches rather than one-piece flow. Waiting is often caused by decoupled operations. Waste of motion indicates problems of parts presentation.

④レイアウト
1人作業の1個流しレイアウトと比較することで、現状のレイアウト上の問題を顕在化させることができる。

④ Layout
Comparing the current layout with one-piece layout for one operator helps you to reveal problems in the current layout.

覚えておこう！ Remember!

生産管理板は、必須の改善ツール The Production Analysis Board Is an Invaluable Tool

生産管理板とは、時間単位に出来高の計画と実績を表示した掲示板です。セル（またはライン）の出口に、必ず設置しなければなりません。

A Production Analysis Board is a display that should be located at the exit of the cell or line, to show actual performance compared with planned performance on an hourly basis.

Production Analysis Board

Cell/Line: **Fuel Line Cell** | Team Leader: **Mary Smith**

Quantity Required: **690 p** | Takt Time: **40 sec.**

Time	Hourly Plan/Actual	Cumulative Plan/Actual	Problems/Causes	Sign-off
06:00~07:00	90/90	90/90		
07:00~08:00	90/88	180/178	Tester failure	
08:00~09:10	90/90	270/268		
09:10~10:10	90/85	360/353	Tester failure	
10:10~11:10	90/90	450/443		
11:40~12:40	90/90	540/533		
12:40~13:40	90/86	630/619	Bad Parts (valves)	
13:50~14:30	60/60	690/679		
O.T.	11/11	690/690	(8 minutes)	
	/	/		
	/	/		
	/	/		

タクトタイムを必ず書く
Don't forget to include the takt time!

Remember breaks

Supervisor signs hourly

Area manager signs at lunch and end of shift

出来高のバラツキの背後には、何らかの問題が存在する！
Fluctuating output is evidence of some hidden problems!

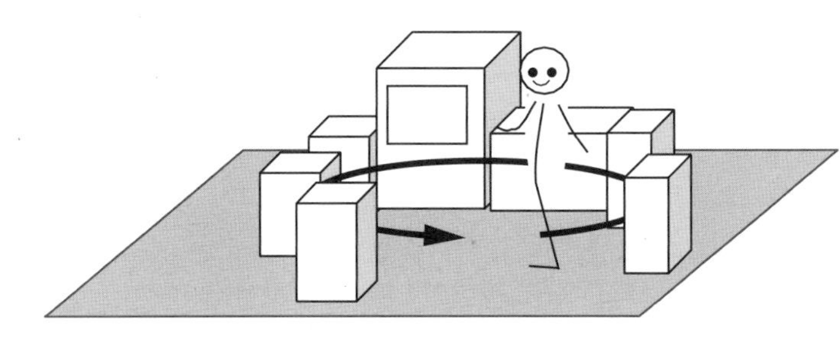

1人完結なら、どんなレイアウト？

How can the physical processes be laid out so one operator can make one piece as efficiently as possible?

Let's talk

U字型の意味
Why a U-shape?

A: 先週は、ブライト工業の工場を見学するチャンスがあって、いろいろなU字セルをたくさん見ました。U字には、どんな意味があるの？

A: Last week, I had the chance to do a plant walk-through at Bright Industries and saw many various U-shaped cells. What advantages does the U-shape provide?

B: ライン設計にあたって、１人完結で最初から最後までつくると仮定して、一筆書きができるように、設備、作業台、部品供給治具を配置してみる。実際にはそういう運用をしないとしても、ね。

B: When you design the line, you arrange the machines, workstations, and parts presentation devices in a series of processing steps, as if only one operator makes the product from beginning to end, even if you will never run the line with one operator.

A: 確かに、離れ小島も避けられる、工程間の停滞も抑えられる、歩行のムダもないし、動作線上の障害物もない、作業者は付加価値を生まない作業から開放される…、というようなラインを、自動的に設計できるわ。だから、多くのセルが、おのずと狭いU字型になるのですね。

A: In this way, I can automatically design a line that avoids isolated islands, minimizes inventory accumulation between steps, eliminates excessive walking, removes obstacles on the walking paths, and frees the operator from non-value-creating work. So, many cells naturally end up in a tight U-shape.

B: もちろん、ラインのレイアウトは、製品、設備、部品供給方法などに影響されるものです。ですから、実際には、さまざまな形のラインが可能です。大切なのは、セルの出口を、できるだけ入口に近づけることなんだよ。

B: Of course, the line layout is often affected by the products, the equipment, and parts presentation issues so various different shapes are possible. But don't forget: it is important to locate the exit of the cell as close as possible to the entrance.

ジャスト・イン・タイム — 3
Just-in-Time with Flow, Pull, and Heijunka

後工程引き取り

Pull—Do Not Push Anything, Anywhere, at Any Time

押し込みはいけない

他の多くのTPS用語と同じように、「後工程引き取り」もまた、「いつでもどこでも何でも、押し込みはいけない！」という基本的な考え方を意味する場合と、手法のセットをさす場合の、２つの使われ方があることに注意しましょう。

考え方としての「後工程引き取り」
後工程引き取りとは、お客様、つまり自工程にとっての後工程が必要とするものを、必要な時に、必要な分だけ、後工程からの何らかの「信号」に従って、供給するということです。引き取りの反対は「押し込み(プッシュ)」です。モノを後工程へ押し込むことは、つくりすぎのムダをつくりだすものです。

Don't Push!

As with many other TPS terms, the word "pull" refers to both a concept — meaning "don't push anything, anywhere, at any time" — and a set of techniques.

Pull concept
Pull means providing the customer or following process with what is needed when it is needed in the right quantity, according to a "signal" from the customer process. The opposite of pull is push, where previous processes push what they produce onto following customer processes. Pushing things to the following process causes overproduction.

後工程引き取りとは

ジャスト・イン・タイムを支える引き取り
後工程引き取りは、ジャスト・イン・タイムを支える主要な３要素の３つ目です。３要素とは、タクトタイム、流れ化、そして後工程引き取りです。先の２つに加えて、後工程引き取りがきちんとできてくると、つくりすぎを抑え、すべてのプロセスの棚卸しを低減することができるのです。

What Is a Pull System?

A pull system to support just-in-time
A pull system is the third of three major elements that compose just-in-time (along with takt time and continuous flow). A well-devised pull system, in addition to the other two elements, can prevent overproduction and reduce the inventory in every process.

押し込みがつくりすぎを生む！
Pushing Things Downstream Causes Overproduction!

後工程の人が引く ······ Starting from the customer downstream

後工程引き取りでは、後工程が前工程に、情報を渡します。このとき、いわゆる「かんばん」がよく使われます。

In a pull system, downstream operations provide information to upstream operations, often via a kanban card.

かんばんは目で見る管理の道具 ······ Kanban is a visual tool to run a pull system

引き取り方式を実現するためには、前工程に対して生産の指示を与えたり、みずすましに対して引き取りの指示を出したりするための、誰にでもわかるような、何らかの道具が必要です。かんばんは、このような伝達手段の中で、最もよく知られ、また最も一般的なものです。

In a pull system, we need some sort of signaling device that gives instructions to upstream suppliers for production, or to the material handlers for withdrawal. Kanban cards are the best-known and most common of these signaling devices.

最終製品をどうつくる？スーパーマーケットor受注生産

How Do You Produce Your Finished Goods? Supermarket or Build to Order (BTO)?

あなたが現在取り組んでいるテーマが上流工程の改善だとしても、それを全体の改善へとつなげるためには、最終製品をどのようにつくるのかということが、まず決まっていなければなりません。どこの改善であれ、あらゆる改善は、お客様に最も近い最下流（出荷場ないし最終組立ライン）を起点とし、「後工程はお客様」という精神で上流工程へと展開すべきなのです。

Before you try to improve your upstream processes, your scheduling method to produce finished goods should be defined first of all. Ordinarily, kaizen should begin at the process closest to your customer (shipping or final assembly) and should be expanded back to upstream processes in a spirit of "the following process is the customer of each supplying process."

スーパーマーケット方式（在庫を持つ） ……………… **Supermarket pull system**

最も基本的、共通的な方式です。スーパーマーケットは、単なる製品の置き場ではなく、お客様が製品を引き取ったら、その分だけ補充し、在庫を一定の量に保つ機能を持ちます。「A タイプのプル」とも言います。

The supermarket system is the most basic and most common type of pull system. A supermarket is not only a storage place, but creates pull by requiring replenishment or by plugging gaps created in the finished goods store when the customer withdraws product. Supermarket pull is sometimes referred to as "A-type pull."

受注生産（在庫を持たない） ……………………………… **Building directly to shipping**

「B タイプのプル」とも言います。顧客からの注文頻度が低く、顧客が望むリードタイムが、ペースメーカー工程から出荷までのリードタイムよりも長いときに使う方法です。A タイプよりも棚卸しを低く抑えることができますが、安定した流れと短いリードタイムが必須です。

Building directly to shipping is part of what is sometimes referred to as "B-type pull," often used when order frequency is low and customer lead-time is longer than your lead-time from pacemaker to delivery. It can keep the inventory at lower levels than A-type pull, but the reliability of your stream and shorter lead-time are crucial!

ワンポイントレッスン One-Point Advice

運搬がペースをつくる

トヨタ生産方式では、運搬は、流れにペースを与える重要な機能とされています。

運搬は、単にモノを運ぶだけのものではありません。運搬それ自体が生産指示となり、また異常を見つける働きをすることが求められます。

Conveyance Should Set the Pace!

In TPS, conveyance provides the important function of giving a ***pace*** to the production flow.

Conveyance does much more than just deliver things. Conveyance itself should become a production instruction, and perform as a checker on abnormalities in workplaces.

定量運搬と定時運搬

みずすましによる少量定時多頻度運搬を採用する工場が増えています。しかし、故・大野耐一氏が、戦後間もないトヨタの機械工場で引き取りを始めたときには、文字通り「後工程の人が、要るときに、要るものを、要るだけ、前工程へ取りに行く」という定量不定期運搬であったことを忘れてはいけないでしょう。運搬を設計するときは、まず、あなた自身が引き取りに行くことから始めるべきです。あなた自身が実際に引き取りをやってみれば、多くの発見があることに驚くはずです。そして、現実をより深く理解した上で、運搬を設計することができるようになるのです。

Two Methods of Conveyance: Fixed-Quantity and Fixed-Time

Mizusumashi (water-spider) methods are now common in many plants around the world. However, the original pull system was a simple fixed-quantity-and-unfixed-time-based withdrawal method where a person from the following process would go to the supplying process by him/herself to pick up the items needed at the time they were needed in the amount needed. When you design your conveyance systems, start by going to withdraw items yourself! You will be surprised by what you discover and will be able to design a much better conveyance system based on your understanding.

Discussion Point	How to Convey	
	Fixed-Quantity, Unfixed-Time	Fixed-Time, Unfixed-Quantity
Inventory	Supplier must adapt to variable times	Supplier must adapt to variable quantities
Withdrawal time	Variable	Fixed
Quantity withdrawn	Fixed	Variable
Usage	✓ Processes connected as a virtual flow ✓ Short conveyance distances ✓ Large lots upstream	✓ Disconnected processes ✓ Job shop layout ✓ Long-distance conveyance

覚えておこう！ Remember!

スーパーマーケットのルーツはアメリカ

アメリカにはスーパーマーケットというものがあると知った大野耐一氏は、その考えを製造に活かして、1953年に初めて機械工場で「スーパーマーケット」をつくり、引き取りを始めました。やがて1956年に大野氏は米国を訪れますが、数々の大きな工場よりもスーパーマーケットが最も印象深かったと後に回顧しています。

An Idea from U.S. Supermarkets

Taiichi Ohno heard about supermarkets in the U.S. in the middle of the 1940s and tried to apply its idea to the production line. In 1953, Ohno set up the first supermarket in Toyota's machine shop and began pull production. In 1956, he visited the U.S. He reflected later that the (U.S.) supermarkets he visited at that time were more impressive for him than the big American factories he visited then.

スーパーマーケットは、つくった工程のすぐ近くに置くべし
Locate Your Supermarket as Close as Possible to the Supplying Process!

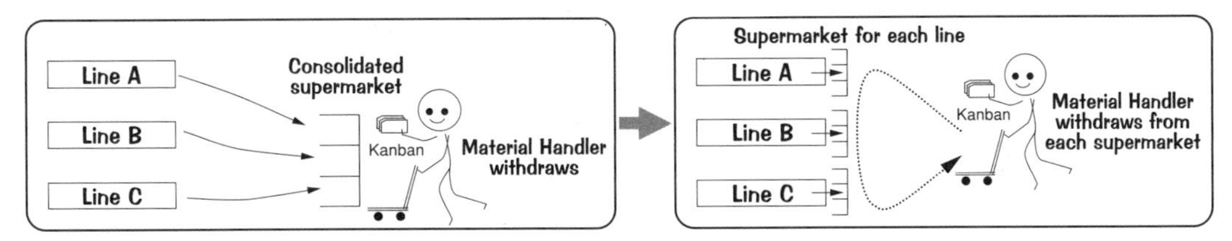

Let's talk スーパーマーケットをつくる
Making a supermarket system

A: 先週、実践会でサブアセンブリ工程のスーパーマーケットをつくりました。アドバイスをお願いします。

A: Last week, we held a kaizen session and made a supermarket at the subassembly line. Would you please give us some advice to improve it?

B: 固定ロケーションにして、在庫の最大量を決めたんだね。これはよいと思います。しかし、つくったところから、遠過ぎるね。

B: You employed fixed-location and determined the maximum quantity for each item, didn't you? It is the right way to make a supermarket. But it is too far from the lines.

A: 遠過ぎるのですね？　それはわかっているのですが、ラインは3本あります。スーパーマーケットはどこに置けばよいのでしょうか？

A: Too far? We know that, but we have three subassembly lines. Where should we place the supermarket?

B: それぞれのラインのすぐ近くに、1つずつスーパーマーケットをつくるんです。みずすましは各ラインから引き取ります。

B: You had better set up one supermarket very close to each line. The material handler will withdraw items from each supermarket.

A: みずすましの仕事が増えてしまいます。

A: It will cause extra work for the material handler.

B: スーパーマーケットの目的は、離れた工程間を流れでつなぐこと、問題を素早く見つけて対策を実行することにあります。みずすましに過重な負担を強いることを避けるのはよいとしても、みずすましの仕事を減らすこと自体が目的ではありません。

B: Our objective with supermarkets is to connect processes that are physically disconnected as a flow, and to identify and solve problems more quickly. It may be better to avoid severe burden on material handlers, but reducing a material handler's work itself is not our main objective.

A: なるほど、ラインのすぐ近くに置けば、誰が不良をつくったのか、よくわかりますね。

A: Okay. I can see that locating supermarkets closer to each line will help us to identify which line makes defects.

ジャスト・イン・タイム — 4
Just-in-Time with Flow, Pull, and Heijunka

モノの置き方
Placing Things to Eliminate Waste

モノの置き方でムダを取る

The Way We Place Things and Organize the Workplace Can Make It Easy to See Waste

現場で、モノをどのように置くかということは、きわめて重要です。モノとは、完成品、仕掛品、部品、材料、棚、作業台、椅子、トレー、梱包資材、さまざまな工具や図面などのこと。

How to place things in the workplace is crucial. "Things" here means finished goods, work-in-process, parts, materials, shelves, workstations, chairs, containers, packaging materials, various tools or documents, etc.

流れの目をもって工場を歩けば、モノのほとんどが、付加価値を付けられるでもなく、単に置かれているだけだということに、すぐに気づくでしょう。
停滞は、すべてムダなのです。
さらに、部品や治具の置き方が悪いと、動作のムダや、不良をつくるムダを引き起こしてしまいます。

When you walk through your plant with "eyes for flow," you will find soon that most material is simply stagnant without value being added. Any stagnation is waste.
In addition, incorrect parts presentation or tool placement often cause the waste of motion and the waste of making defects.

ですから、モノを置くときは、ムダを取るように置くことが大切なのです。

- ムダが見える置き方
- 停滞をなくす置き方
- 動作のムダやミスをなくす置き方

So, you should place things to eliminate waste as below:

- Visible presentation
- Preventing stagnation
- Eliminating the waste of motion and defects

Set in Order (整頓)—A Place for Everything and Everything in Its Place

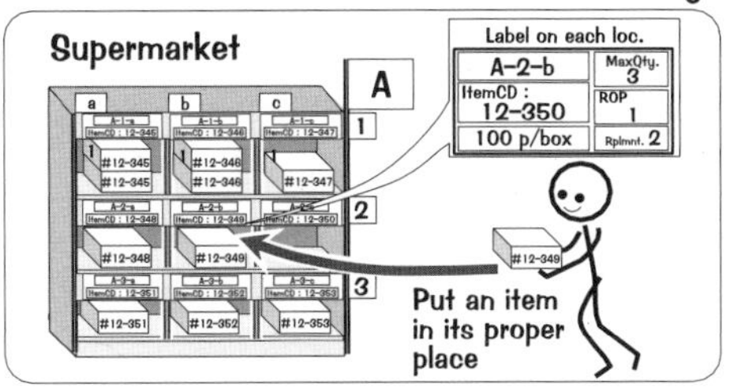

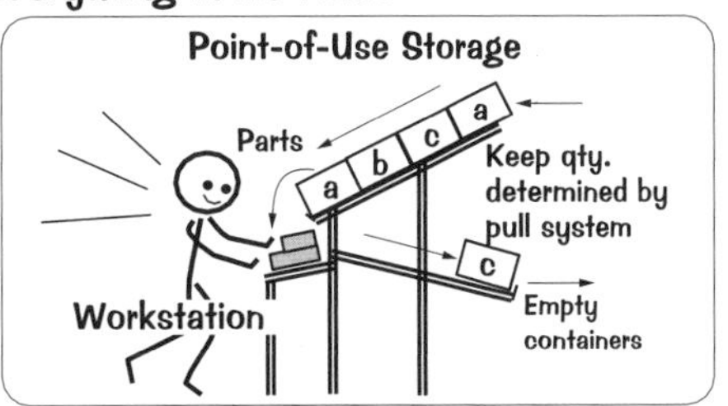

5Sは改善の基本

Five S Is a Foundation of Kaizen

5Sとは

5Sとは、Sで始まる次の5つの用語からなる、一見すると簡単そうに見えるシステムのこと。5Sは、改善の基盤です。

Five Ss (5S)

5Ss is a deceptively simple system composed of five related terms beginning with an S sound as below. It is the foundation of Kaizen.

整理

要るモノと要らないモノを分けて、要らないモノを捨てる。

Sort out ["Seiri" in Japanese]

Separate needed from unneeded things and discard the unneeded.

整頓

要るモノだけを、使いやすいように、使う順に並べる。

Set in order ["Seiton" in Japanese]

Arrange items that are needed in a neat and easy-to-use manner and in sequence of use or consumption.

清掃

きれいに掃除するのみならず、現場に何か異常がないか、点検することでもある。

Shine (and inspect) ["Seiso" in Japanese]

The third S means not only sweeping up the work area, or cleaning equipment, but also inspection of anything abnormal at the work area.

清潔

整理・整頓・清掃の3Sが保たれた状態。清潔とは、「汚すな」でもある。

Spic-and-span ["Seiketsu" in Japanese]

The overall cleanliness and order that result from disciplined practice of the first three Ss. It also means "Don't litter the work area!"

しつけ(躾)

4Sが身に付いていること。

Sustain ["Sitsuke" in Japanese]

Sustain the first four Ss. Sometimes referred to as "discipline."

キレイの基準を決める　The Third S —"Shine(Seiso)"

5Sについて、多くの企業が特に最初の2つのS、整理・整頓に力を入れています。しかし、3つ目のS、すなわち清掃も、とても大切なしつけの一つです。それぞれの現場ごとに、「キレイとは何か」をはっきりと定義し、説明しなければなりません。そして、全員を3Sに巻き込むのです！

Many companies focus their 5S exercises on the first two Ss — Sort and Set in Order. But the third S — Shine — is also an important basic discipline. We should develop a clear definition and explanation of what shine means at every gemba and get everyone engaged in 3S activities!

「キレイにする」とは？

- 何を清掃するのか？
- どのように清掃するのか？
- 誰が清掃するのか？
- いつ、何回清掃するのか？
- どのくらいキレイにするのか？

We have to define our "Shine":

- What to clean?
- How to clean?
- Who will do the cleaning?
- How often to clean?
- How clean is clean?

覚えておこう！ Remember!

1個、2個と数えられる製品の改善では、入り数（収容数）とピッチを覚えておくと便利です。

Improvement of countable items should be related to pack-out quantity and pitch.

Takt Time × Pack-Out Quantity = Pitch

60 sec./p ×  20 p/container = 20 minutes

ワンポイントレッスン One-Point Advice

ラインの中にモノを置く

Placing Things for Efficient Production

ここでは、ムダをとるための部品や仕掛品、設備の置き方を説明します。

The following shows how to place materials, WIP, and machines to eliminate waste.

動作のムダをとる置き方

- 左右の手はそれぞれ同時並行。
- 一度に両手を使うなら、可能な限り、その動作を小さく。
- 軽作業なら、肩や上腕を動かさず、両手の範囲または前腕の範囲で。
- 作業者の動きは、滑らかに、流れるように。
- 作業者の前に最小限の半円を描き、その中で作業ができるように。ムリな姿勢をさせない。
- できるだけ、作業者の手を空ける。

Economy of motion

- Each hand-movement should be concurrent.
- Two-handed motion should be as compact as possible.
- Light work should be done with the hands and forearms, rather than the upper arms and shoulders.
- Motion should flow freely.
- Work should be done in a half-circle as small as possible in diameter in front of the operator. Maintain appropriate posture.
- Keep hands free as much as possible.

ラインのレイアウトと設備の置き方

- 「売れ」に合わせて、あるいは作業者の身長に合わせて、配置を変えられるように。
- 部品は水平に搬送。垂直方向の動きは避ける。
- 重力を活用して部品を動かす(流れ棚など)。
- 人の動きと設備に合わせて、時計回りか、反時計回りかを決める。

Equipment layout

- Build flexibility into the layout to accommodate demand changes and taller or shorter operators.
- Move parts horizontally. Avoid vertical part movement.
- Use gravity to move parts (e.g., with sloping parts racks).
- Make a choice between clockwise or counterclockwise to meet operators' motion and machines.

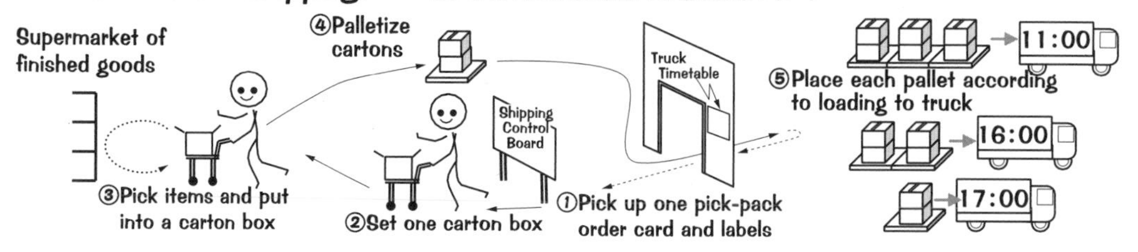

Let's talk　まずは出荷場から始めよう！ Let's start from shipping!

A: 以前の実践会で、改善は出荷場から始めるべしと教えられましたよね。ここが出荷場です。

A: In a previous kaizen session you told us to start from shipping. This is our shipping area.

B: ピッキング作業者が製品を回転式自動倉庫から出して、梱包作業者が梱包しているんだね。出荷便は1日に何回？　ピッキング件数と出荷件数は日当たりで何件？

B: Packing operators pack products picked by pickers from carousels. How often does the truck leave per day? How many picking and shipping orders do you process per day?

A: 3便で、11:00、16:00、17:00発です。ピッキング件数は約400件、出荷は100件です。梱包のタクトは、4分48秒です。

A: The truck leaves three times every day, at 11 a.m., 4 p.m., and 5 p.m. We receive about 400 picking orders per day and about 100 shipping orders per day. So our packing takt time is 4 minutes and 48 seconds.

B: ピッキングから梱包、出荷まで、多工程持ちにすれば、4、5人ですべて出荷できると思うよ。今ここには、10人以上いるよね？

B: In that case, I think four or five operators will be able to process all orders through multi-process-handling from picking-packing to shipping. Over ten operators are working here now, aren't they?

A: すごいわ！　すぐにやってみます。それでは、梱包した製品は、どう置けばよいの？

A: Great! We'll try it from now on. And then, how should we palletize packed products?

B: まず、トラックの時刻表を出口の壁に貼ること。それから、トラックごとに、今日の出荷オーダーを積載順に並べてリストをつくる。それを出荷管理板に貼るんだよ。

B: Put up a truck-timetable board first on the wall at the exit. Next, compile a list of today's shipping orders in sequence of palletizing and loading to each truck, and post the lists on a Shipping Control Board.

A: わかったわ！　そのリストの順に、梱包済みのモノを置くのですね。

A: I got it! We'll place packed products according to those lists on the Board.

ジャスト・イン・タイム — 5
Just-in-Time with Flow, Pull, and Heijunka

かんばん
What Is Kanban?

かんばんは、後工程引き取りの道具

日本国内では、かんばん＝トヨタ生産方式 ではない、ということが、広く理解されるようになりました。しかし、トヨタ生産方式＝ジャスト・イン・タイム＝かんばん、と捉えている人もいるでしょう。そこで、かんばんについて話すときは、常に、２本柱、タクトタイム、流れ化などの構造やセオリー、「かんばんは、後工程引き取りの道具、改善の道具」であること、等々を復習してから、かんばんそのものの話題に入るようにするのがよいでしょう。同じ話の繰返しはムダでは？とも思うでしょうが、これらの基本を繰り返し教え、また学ぶことは、チームにもあなた自身にも、より深い理解をもたらすということが、だんだん分かってくるはずです。

かんばんとは
かんばんとは、後工程引き取りにおいて、生産したり、引き取ったりしてよいという許可を与えたり、あるいは生産や引き取りをしなさいという指示を出したりする、ある種の信号のようなもの。引き取りとは、後工程からの要求に基づく運搬。

Kanban: a Pull System Tool

In Japan, it has become well-known that kanban is not the same thing as the Toyota Production System. However, some people still tend to think kanban is exactly the same as just-in-time or even TPS. Therefore, we should always begin explanations of kanban after reviewing the structure and theory of the two pillars of TPS, as well as all of the elements of just-in-time: takt time, continuous flow, and a pull system (i.e., replenishment production) enabled by kanban as a tool. You may sometimes find it tedious to repeat the same lessons over and over, but you will see that the repetition of teaching and learning these basics will bring deeper understanding for your team members and you!

What is kanban?
A kanban is a signaling device that gives authorization and instruction for the production or withdrawal of items in a pull system. "Withdrawal" means the conveyance called on by the downstream operation.

かんばんの具体像

Kanban Particulars

かんばんカード(普通にかんばんと言えばこれ) ······ **Kanban card**

カード型のかんばんは、後工程からの引きを伝える道具のうちで、最もよく知られ、また最もよく使われているものです。長方形の伝票のようなもので、ときに透明なビニールケースに入っています。一般的にかんばんに記載されるのは、

- 部品名と部品番号
- つくった人(ベンダーまたは社内の工程名)
- 収容数(入り数)
- ストアの所番地
- 使用する工程の所番地
- 引き取りのサイクル

(バーコードが印刷されていることもある)

Kanban cards are the best-known and most common examples of pull signals. They often are small cards, sometimes protected in clear vinyl envelopes, that provide information such as:

- Part name and part number
- Supplier or internal supplying process
- Pack-out quantity
- Storage address
- Consuming process address
- How often it is to be withdrawn

(A bar code may be printed on the card.)

かんばんのいろいろな形 ······························ **Various types of kanban**

カードのほかにも、かんばんには、三角形の金属板や色付きボール、トレーそれ自体や電子的な信号などがあり、また、誤った指示を出すことなく、必要な情報だけを伝えることができるものなら何であれ、かんばんとして使うことができます。

Besides cards, kanban can be triangular metal plates, colored balls, containers themselves, electronic signals, or any other device that can convey the needed information, *and only the needed information* (cancelling out the noise of unneeded information).

かんばんの種類　Types of Kanban

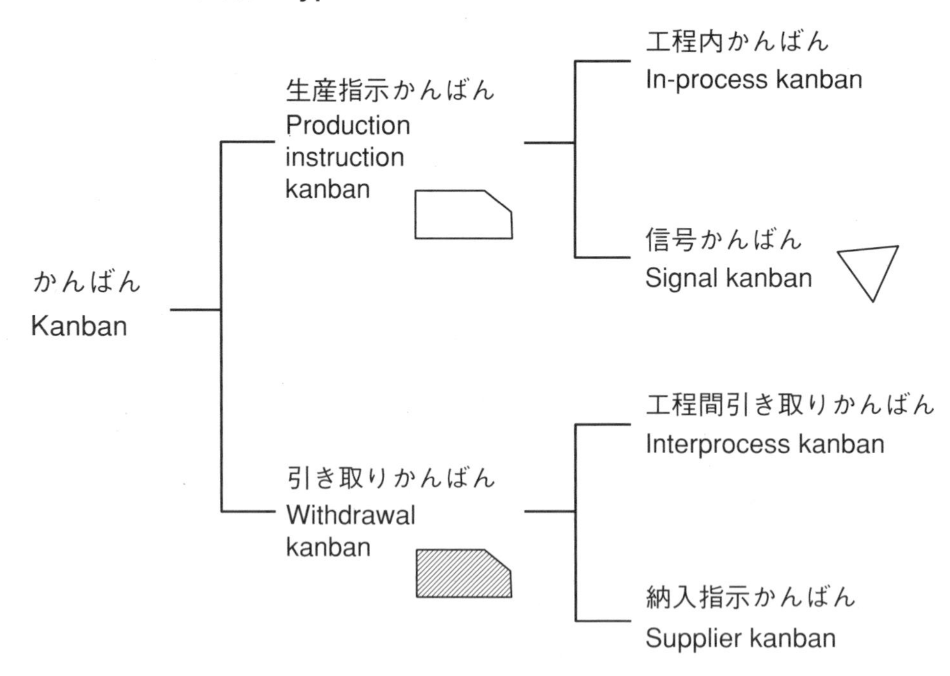

生産指示かんばんと引き取りかんばん
Example of Production Kanban and Withdrawal Kanban

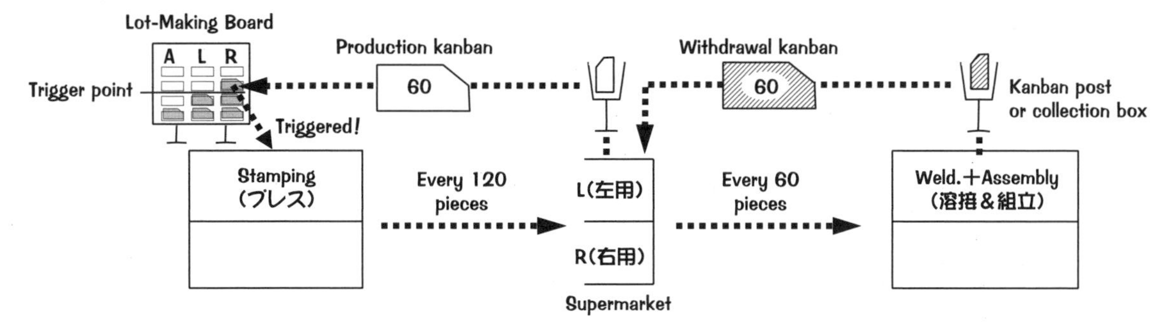

生産指示かんばんと、引き取りかんばん

Production Instruction Kanban and Withdrawal Kanban

皆さんが働く工場には、いろいろなかんばんがあることでしょう。しかし、初めのうちは、名称や形にはあまりこだわらず、「かんばんは、その機能から大きく２つに分類でき、それぞれにさまざまなかんばんがあり得る」と説明した方が、後の理解のためには役立ちます。

You may already have various forms of kanban in some of your plants. In the initial stages, however, it is better to stick with the basics, saving more detailed explanations for later. Kanban are categorized into two major groups, as explained below.

かんばんの２つの機能

その形状がどんなものであれ、かんばんは、製造において、２つの機能を持っています。つまり、製品や部品をつくりなさいと指示する機能と、運搬担当者に対して製品や部品を運びなさいと指示する機能です。前者を生産指示かんばん、後者を引き取りかんばんと呼びます。

Kanban have two functions

Whatever the form, kanban have two functions in a production operation: They instruct processes to make products or parts, and they instruct material handlers to move products or parts. The former use is called production kanban; the latter use is termed withdrawal kanban.

生産指示かんばん

生産指示かんばんは、前工程に対して、後工程のために、どの製品（または部品）を、いくつつくりなさい、と伝えるものです。

Production kanban

Production kanban (or “make cards”) tell a supplying process the type and quantity of products (or parts) to make for a downstream process.

引き取りかんばん

引き取りかんばんは、製品（や部品）を後工程へ運んでよろしいという許可を与えます。工場内の「工程間引き取りかんばん」と、外部との間で使う「納入指示かんばん」の２種類があります。

Withdrawal kanban

Withdrawal kanban (or “move cards”) authorize the conveyance of products (or parts) to a downstream process. They often take two forms: internal (or interprocess) kanban and supplier kanban.

ワンポイントレッスン One-Point Advice

かんばんのルールは6つ

ほぼ定番表現になっているのですが、TPSの原典（複数）編纂の歴史的経緯と、英語圏におけるTPS研究進展の経緯から、微妙に異なる複数の英語版「6つのルール」が存在しています。皆さんの中には、「どれが正しいのか？」と質問されて困惑した経験のある方もいらっしゃるのでは。順序や表現も大切ですが、まずは考え方をきちんと理解してもらうことを第一としましょう。ここでは、故・大野耐一氏の「トヨタ生産方式」をもとにした近年の英訳表現を紹介します。

①お客様である後工程は、かんばんが外れた分だけ、前工程から引き取る。（これを物理的に実現するには、いろいろな方法があります。例えば、お客様である後工程の作業者が常に自分で引き取りに行くようにしてもよいし、みずすましの運搬担当者が前工程へ引き取りに行きなさいとかんばんで指示される等々。しかし、いずれにせよ、基本的なルールは同じです。）

②前工程は、かんばんが外れたものを、外れた分だけ、外れた順につくる。

③かんばんがないときは、つくらない、運ばない。

④かんばんは、現物に必ず付けておく（または、モノには、必ずかんばんを付ける）。

⑤不良品を絶対に後工程へ送らない。

⑥かんばんの枚数を減らしていく。

Six Rules for Using Kanban Effectively

Several slightly different versions of the Six Kanban Rules have come into existence as TPS has diffused around the world. This can lead to confusion and the question, “Which version is best?” The order and expression of the rules are important, but first we need to cover the basic concept. The following six rules are from a recent translation based on Taiichi Ohno’s *Toyota Production System* (originally published in Japan in 1978 and translated into English in 1988).

① Customer processes withdraw items in the precise amounts specified on the kanban. (There are various methods that can be used to physically accomplish this—for example, the worker in the customer process may go to withdraw items always by him/herself, or a water-spider material handler may be sent via kanban etc.—but the basic rule stays the same.)

② Supplier processes produce items in the precise amounts and sequence specified by the kanban.

③ No items are made or moved without a kanban.

④ A kanban should always accompany each item. (Each item always has a kanban attached.)

⑤ Defects and incorrect amounts are never sent to the downstream process.

⑥ The number of kanban is reduced carefully to lower inventories and to reveal problems.

おさわり2回

Try to Touch Each Item No More than Two Times!

「おさわり２回」、まさに言うは易く行うは難し、ですね。LEIの教材では、次の表現が紹介されています（"Making Materials Flow"より）。

The Lean Enterprise Institute (LEI) workbook *Making Materials Flow* tells us the following:

Eliminate Triple Handling of Materials

Material handlers should move the materials as directly as possible from the truck to the purchased-parts market, eliminating one or more unnecessary steps while improving quality and accuracy. ··· Of course, in a perfect world, deliveries would go directly from the dock to the value-creating cells in one step. Unfortunately this is rarely possible···.

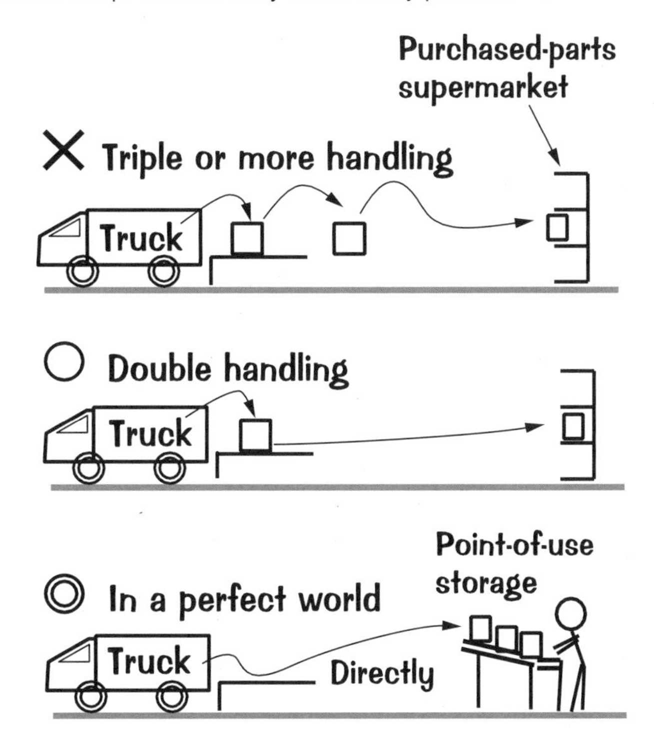

How Often Should the Upstream Supplying Process Fabricate Parts?

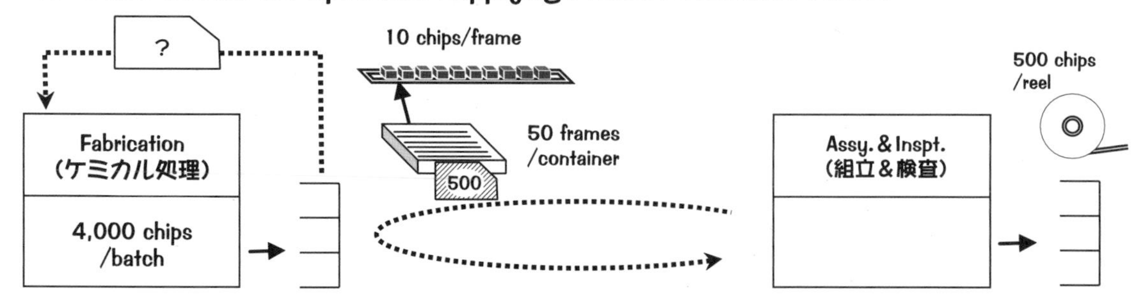

Let's talk 前工程へ引きを伝える
Pace your supplying processes!

A: 最終組立は、前工程のスーパーマーケットから1トレーずつ引き取ります。1トレーには50フレーム、1フレームにはチップ10個が載っています。組立・検査の後、500チップずつ1本のテープリールに巻かれます。

A: The final assembly process withdraws one container at a time from the supermarket. One container contains 50 frames, with ten chips on one frame. After assembly and inspection, they will be combined into 500-chip tape reels.

B: 加工後のチップは何種類ですか？

B: How many types do you have in the chip market?

A: チップは5種類です。でも、前工程の化学処理工程では、500チップずつつくっていたのでは、段取り時間が長過ぎて、必要な量をつくれません。チップの生産指示を、どのように出せばよいでしょう？

A: Five types of chips. But when we make 500 chips at a time in the upstream chemical process, we cannot make enough chips in the quantity needed by the customer process, because changeover-time is too long. How should we trigger the production of chips?

B: 500個ずつつくるのは、今はまだ現実的ではありませんね。ロット生産指示板を使って、4,000個ずつつくることにしようか。

B: It is not practical just yet to make 500 chips at a time. You could set the Lot-Making Board at the beginning process and make 4,000 chips at a time.

A: スーパーマーケットの各トレーに生産指示かんばんを付けて、ロット生産指示板との間で回すのね。それでは、ロット生産指示板の発注点は、いくつにすべきなのかしら？

A: Okay. We'll attach one production kanban on every container at the supermarket, and circulate the kanban between the supermarket and the Lot-Making Board. But, how should we set the trigger point on the Board?

B: 後工程の必要数、化学処理プロセスのロットサイズとリードタイムから発注点を決めるんだ。

B: You can get it from three pieces of information: the quantity needed by the customer process, the lot size, and the lead time of the chemical process.

ジャスト・イン・タイム — 6
Just-in-Time with Flow, Pull, and Heijunka

平準化
What Is Heijunka?

平準化はトヨタ生産方式の大前提

平準化とは、「売れ」に合わせて、生産量と機種をともに均す(ならす)こと。そのまま英語にすると"level(平らにする)"ですが、「量と種類をともに」を理解してもらうために、テクニカル・タームとして、あえて日本語の"heijunka"を使うことをお勧めします。平準化は、トヨタ生産方式の大前提。ほかの手法を解説する時と同様に、平準化も、トヨタ生産方式のゴールや2本柱について復習してから説明するとよいでしょう。

平準化とは
平準化とは、生産する量と機種を、ある一定の期間で均すということを意味します。たとえば、午前中にAだけを組み立てて、午後にはBを組み立てる、ということをせず、AとBを小さなバッチで交互につくるのです。

なぜ平準化するのか?
平準化すれば、まとめづくりをせずに、「売れ」に合わせてムダなく生産できるようになり、結果として、モノの流れの全体にわたって、最少の在庫、資金、工数、リードタイムを実現できるのです。

TPS Relies on Heijunka as a Foundation

We use the Japanese word "heijunka" as a technical term of TPS instead of the English word "leveling" to express the importance of leveling both the amount and the mix. TPS relies on heijunka. Before talking about heijunka itself, as with the other individual elements of system, we had better review again the overall structure of TPS—the goals and the two pillars.

What is heijunka?
Heijunka means leveling the type and quantity of production over a fixed period of time. For example, instead of assembling all the type A products in the morning and all the type B products in the afternoon, we would alternate small batches of A and B.

Why should we do heijunka?
Heijunka enables production to efficiently meet customer demands while avoiding batching, resulting in minimum inventories, capital costs, manpower, and production lead time through the whole value stream.

Batch-and-Queue

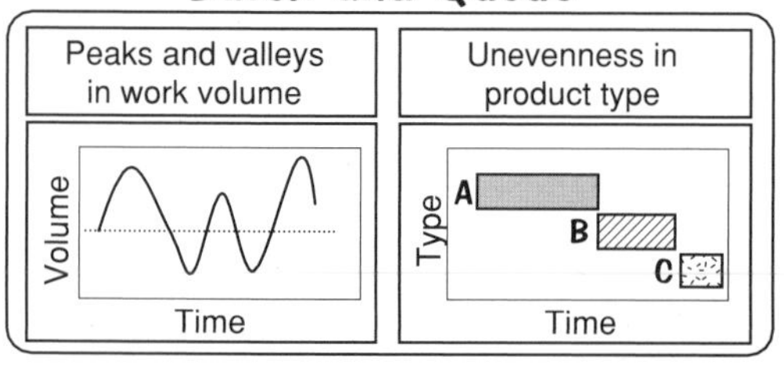

vs.

Heijunka

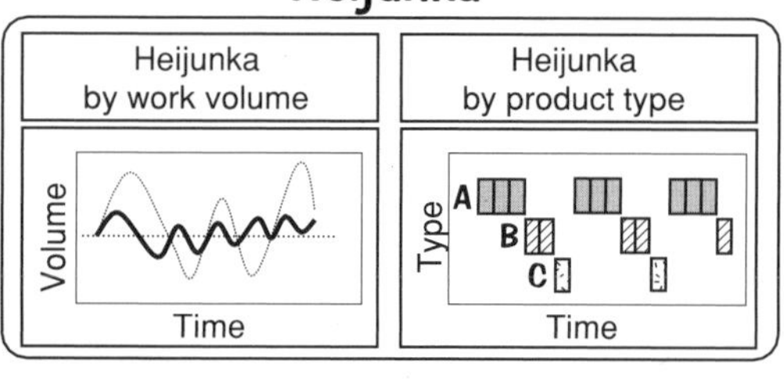

?	Safety	?
?	Quality	?
?	Cost	?
Longer	Lead time	Shorter
Larger	Inventories	Smaller
?	Morale	?

まとめ生産と平準化生産を比べてみよう

Compare *Batch-and-Queue* with *Heijunka*

まとめ生産は効率が良い？

組立部門では、ほとんどの人が、できるだけ長く同じ機種の製品をつくり続け、機種切替えを避けることがよいと考えています。しかし、この方が、結局は高くつくのです。

Is batch production truly efficient?

Many assembly departments think it is easier to schedule long runs of one product type and avoid changeovers. However, they pay heavily in the end.

まとめ生産と平準化生産の意味を簡単に説明した後、「どちらがリードタイムが短いと思いますか？」「在庫水準はどうですか？」「品質はどちらが良くなると思いますか？」「働く人にとっては？」などと問いかけ、自ら考えてもらうことで、さらに理解が深まるはずです。

It is effective to facilitate a group discussion after a basic explanation of heijunka. Ask your team members questions such as: Which is better to shorten lead time: batch-and-queue or heijunka? Which is better to improve inventory levels? Which is better for quality? Which is better for the operators?

リードタイムは？

バッチ生産では、リードタイムは長くなり、今つくっているバッチの機種とは違う機種が欲しいお客様への対応は難しくなります。そして、お客様が求める機種を、常に持っていたいと思うなら、完成品在庫を増やさなければなりません。

How about lead time?

Batch production expands lead times. So it becomes difficult to serve customers who want something different than the batch we are making now. Therefore, we have to invest money in finished goods, hoping that we will have on-hand what the customer wants.

材料や部品は？

まとめてつくるということは、材料も部品もまとめて使うということであり、仕掛品の在庫をふくらませ、サプライヤーにもムラ(仕事量の波)という負担をかけることになります。

How about materials and parts?

Batch production also means that we consume raw materials and parts in batches, which swells WIP inventories and places the burden of mura (unevenness) on suppliers.

品質は？

まとめ生産は不良を覆い隠してしまいます。不良をつくっても、そのバッチをつくっている間(には発見できず)、不良をつくり続けてしまいます。このため、品質が良くならないのです。

How about quality?

Batch production hides defects. Quality suffers because a single defect becomes replicated throughout the batch.

働く人にとっては？

まとめ生産では、作業者は、あるラインはとても忙しいのに、ほかのラインは遊んでいる、というような目に遭います。このやり方はムダが多く、また、仕事にムラがあるとムリが生じ、ムリは安全やモラールも蝕んでしまうのです。

How about the impact on workers?

Workers experience unevenness—that is, some lines are very busy, others idle—which also degrades efficiency. The unevenness in the work creates strain, which corrodes safety and morale.

ワンポイントレッスン One-Point Advice

在庫を持つ機種と受注生産する機種を決める——ABC分析

How to Decide Your Production Scheduling Method—ABC Production Analysis

まとめ生産から平準化生産へ転換するための第1歩は、在庫を持つ機種と受注生産する機種を決めることです。ご存知の通り、ABC分析を基にして決定します。以下に例を挙げます。

To transform your system from batch-and-queue to heijunka, you have to decide the scheduling method you will use to produce finished goods for your customer. First, perform an ABC Production Analysis as shown below. (See the next page.)

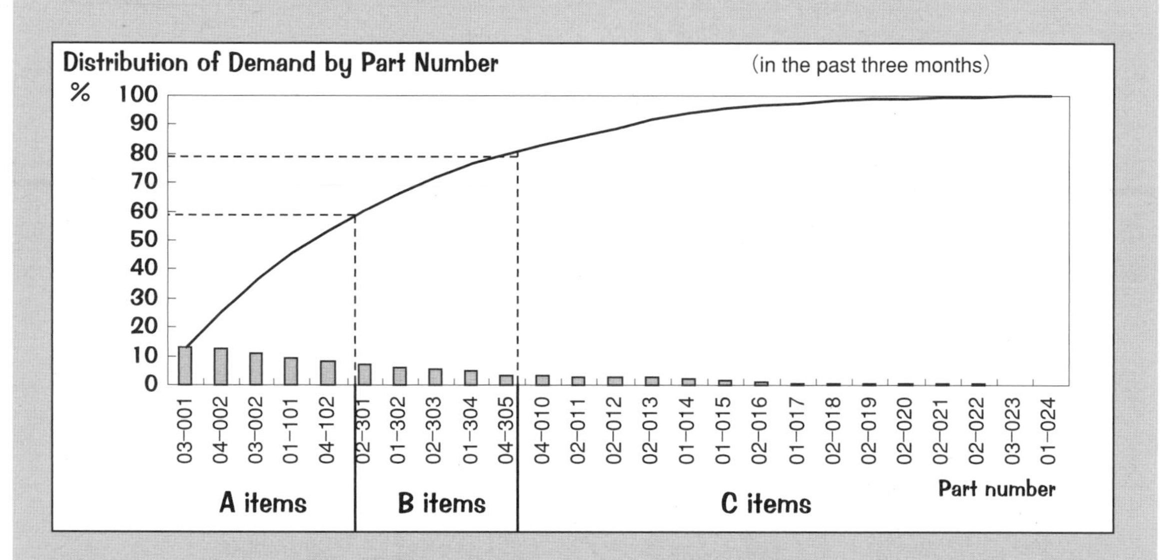

The bars in the diagram show the fraction of total demand accounted for by each part number. The curved line running from left to right stacks the orders to show the fraction of demand accounted for by any given number of products. In the above example, the first five part numbers account for 60% of total demand and the first 10 account for 80%.

A items are high runners, B items are medium runners, and C items are low runners.

Options for Finished Goods vs. Make-to-Order　何を在庫し、何を受注生産するか？

		Options　選択肢	Pros　よい点	Cons　課題
①		Hold finished-goods inventory of all products (As, Bs, and Cs) and make all to stock – **replenishment pull system** **後補充生産**（完成品在庫への後補充）	Ready to ship all items on short notice すべての機種で短納期対応が可能になる	Requires space and inventory of every item 全機種について在庫を持つ必要があり、スペースが必要
②		Hold no finished-goods inventory and make all products to order – **sequential pull system** **順序生産**（在庫を持たず受注生産）	Less inventory and associated waste 在庫と在庫に関連するムダを削減できる	Requires high process stability and short lead time to produce 工程の安定化と、生産リードタイム短縮が求められる
③	ⓐ	Hold only Cs in inventory and make A and B products to order daily – **mixed pull system** **Cは後補充、A，Bを順序生産**	Less inventory 在庫を少なくすることができる	Requires mixed production control and daily stability 後補充＋順序生産のきちんとした管理と、日次の安定化が必要
	ⓑ	Hold A and B products in finished-goods inventory. Make Cs to order from semi-finished components – **mixed pull system** **A，Bは後補充、Cを順序生産**	Moderate inventory 在庫を抑えることができる（①案よりは少ないが、②案よりは多い）	Requires mixed production control and visibility on C items 後補充＋順序生産のきちんとした管理と、Cの見える化が必要

注：
最終製品の在庫の決め方とペースメーカーにおけるスケジューリング手法については、ワークブック Creating Level Pull を参照してください。

Note:
As for the details of the frame and methods how to define the inventories for final goods and scheduling at the pacemaker process, see the LEI workbook *Creating Level Pull*.

How Much of Each Item Should We Hold in Finished Goods?
完成品在庫の量を決める

Finished-goods calculation formula

	Average daily demand × Lead time to replenish (days)	Cycle stock	Finished goods supermarket
+	Demand variation as % of Cycle stock	Buffer stock	
+	Safety factor as % of (Cycle stock + Buffer stock)	Safety stock	
=		Finished-goods inventory	

Tip:Try holding your safety separately from cycle and buffer stock…use it only in emergencies!

Let's talk 平準化に向けて Setting inventory levels for heijunka

A: ABC分析をして、AとBは後補充、Cは受注生産の「組合せ型プル」にすると決めました。また、Cは小さな専用セルでつくることにしました。次はどうすればよいですか？

A: After doing an ABC production analysis, we have decided to employ a mixed pull system and hold finished goods for A and B items. We have also decided on having a dedicated small cell for C items. What should we do next?

B: AとBの完成品在庫の量を決めるんだ。品番ごとに算出する。こんなふうにね(上図)。

B: You have to decide the initial finished-goods inventory levels for A and B. Calculate it for each item in this way (see the above formula).

A: じゃ、計算してみますね。……わぁ！　今まで、在庫をあまりにも多く持ち過ぎていたっていうことが、改めてわかったわ。

A: Okay. … Oh!　I see that we had been keeping too much inventory.

B: わかってくれたかな？　在庫を抑えながら後補充をきちんとするためには、異常がすぐわかるようにすることがとても大切なんだよ。

B: Good, so now you see. It is crucial to make "normal or abnormal" clear, in order to maintain your inventory levels and replenishment.

A: 次は生産の指示をどうするか、ですよね？

A: Now, we have to discuss how to control production, don't we?

B: その通り。まず、「ペースメーカー」の考え方をしっかり理解する必要があるんだよ。

B: That's right. You need to get a fix on the concept of the "pacemaker" first.

A: ペースメーカー？　以前に聞いたことがあるわ。……この場合なら、最終工程の組立検査よね？

A: The pacemaker? Yes, you taught us about that before. … In this case, it must be the final process, assembly and inspection.

ジャスト・イン・タイム — 7
Just-in-Time with Flow, Pull, and Heijunka

1ヵ所だけに生産指示を出す —ペースメーカー

Send the Production Schedule to One Place – the Pacemaker

ペースメーカーだけが生産指示を受け取る

ペースメーカーとは

1つの製品群のバリュー・ストリーム上で、流れの全体に拍動を与えるただ1つの場所のこと。ペースメーカー工程だけが、生産管理部門から生産指示を受け取るのです。

ペースメーカー選定の考え方

ペースメーカー工程は、通常、バリュー・ストリームの最下流の顧客に近い場所です。多くの場合、最終組立工程がこれに該当します。もっと上流の工程をペースメーカーとすることも可能ですが、これは当該上流工程からバリュー・ストリームの最下流まで、先入れ先出しが保たれることを前提とするものです。

注意！　ネック工程とは違う

ペースメーカー工程を、ボトルネック工程と混同してはなりません。

Only the Pacemaker Gets the Production Instructions

What is a pacemaker?

It means a single point along a value stream that sets the pace for the entire stream. Only the pacemaker process receives the schedule from the production control operation.

Which process should we designate?

The pacemaker process usually is near the customer end of the value stream, often the final assembly area. Any upstream process can be a pacemaker, provided that products flow from this upstream process to the end of the value stream in a FIFO (First in, First out) sequence.

Don't be confused!

The pacemaker process should not be confused with a bottleneck process.

伝統的なスケジューリングと、リーンなスケジューリング（後補充生産方式の例）

Traditional Scheduling and Lean Scheduling (An Example of Replenishment Pull)

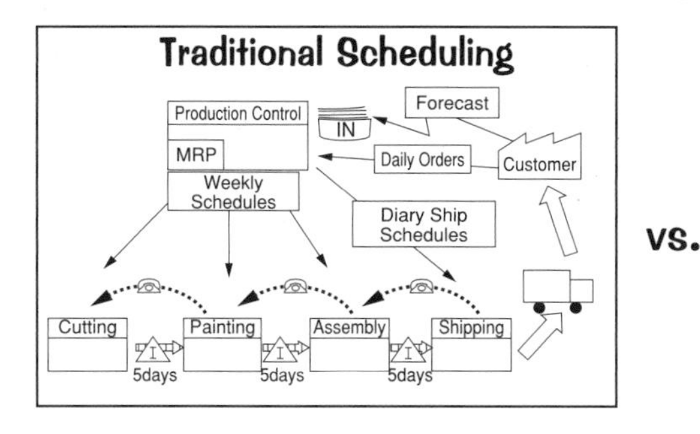

vs.

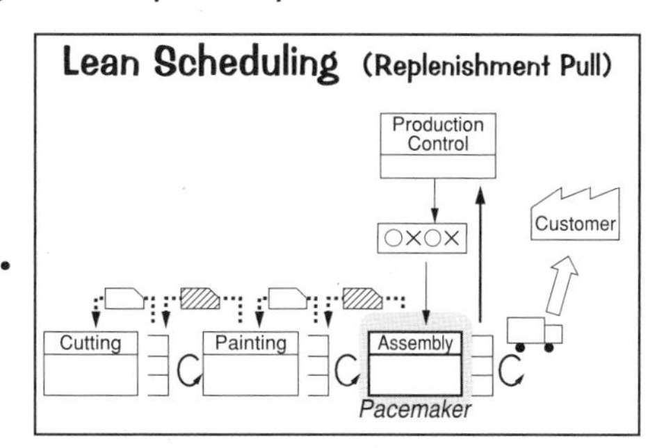

なぜペースメーカー工程を決めるのか？

Why Do We Need a Pacemaker?

伝統的な押し込み生産

MRPのような伝統的なスケジューリングでは、それぞれの工程に対して、いっせいに生産指示を出します。この方法は、どれが正しい計画なのかわからないという混乱を生むとともに、結果としてつくりすぎの原因にもなるものです。

Traditional push

In traditional scheduling, such as MRP, multiple schedules are created and sent directly to each process. This method causes confusion over the "right" schedule and results in overproduction.

1カ所だけに生産指示を出す

ペースメーカー工程を1カ所に決めれば、バリュー・ストリーム上の誰もが1つの同じ拍動――つまりペースメーカーのタクトタイムに合わせて、仕事をすることができるようになります。

Only the pacemaker receives the schedule

Selecting a single point as the pacemaker enables everyone along the value stream to keep working to the same beat—the takt time at the pacemaker.

ペースメーカー工程における バッチサイズ

How to Determine Batch Sizes at the Pacemaker?

先に説明した「平準化」は、ペースメーカー工程に対する生産指示においてこそ、最初になされるべきものなのです。ペースメーカー工程が大バッチのままであったなら、バリュー・ストリーム全体の在庫は、伝統的なまとめと押し込みの時代と大差ないレベルにとどまってしまうでしょう。

Heijunka is applied first at the pacemaker process. If the pacemaker process continues to produce in batches, the inventories along with the entire value stream will remain as high as in a conventional batch-and-push system.

お客様が求める荷姿（収容数）に着目する

収容数とは、運搬と出荷に際し、1コンテナに入れるようお客様が求めている数のことです。ペースメーカーにおけるバッチサイズは、この収容数と同じか、その倍数にすることが目標です。

How much is the customer pack-out quantity?

Pack-out quantity means the number of products that a customer requires packed in a container for transportation and shipping. The goal is to produce at the pacemaker in the same batch size as the pack-out quantity or a multiple of it.

ペースメーカー工程のバッチサイズを決める

理想的なのは、バッチサイズをお客様の収容数の単位と同じにすることです。しかし、段取り時間の長さや、機種間の作業量の差異のために、多くの企業にとって、これは困難です。ペースメーカーのバッチサイズは、下記を慎重に考慮して決めるべきです。

- 作業量の機種間のバラツキ
- 段取り時間
- ピッチ・インターバル

What should be the pacemaker batch size?

An ideal method is to produce products in the same size as the pack-out quantity. But this is very difficult for many processes because of their long changeover times and work content differences between products. It should be determined after carefully evaluating below:

- Work content differences between products
- Changeover times
- Pitch interval

ワンポイントレッスン One-Point Advice

いよいよ平準化！でもその前に

いよいよペースメーカー工程での平準化に挑戦するところまで来ました！　しかし、ちょっと待って下さい。ペースメーカー工程は、流れ化されていなければなりません。ペースメーカー工程をもう一度よく見て、次の２点を確認しましょう。

①流れ化されているか？

ペースメーカー工程は、流れ化されている必要があります。流れ化とは、強制駆動ラインか、または流れ化セル（またはライン）を意味します。これができていないなら、平準化は困難です。１つ戻ってもっと流れ改善に取り組むべきです。

②可動率は75％以上か？

ペースメーカー工程での可動率は、少なくとも75％以上であることが求められます。これができていないなら、まず真因を追究し、問題を解決しなければなりません。

Finally, Try it, but Before Heijunka!

We are now ready to open the door to heijunka at the pacemaker. However, before stepping through that door and making a heijunka production plan, confirm whether or not your pacemaker process is fully prepared. Is it producing in a continuous flow? Is it consistently meeting output requirements? Observe it carefully from these standpoints:

① Has continuous flow been established?

The operations in the pacemaker process should be arranged in a continuous flow. This may mean a moving conveyor line, or a continuous flow cell (or line). If it has been designed poorly, it will be difficult for you to implement a level pull system. In this case, you should take a backward step and make another try at flow kaizen.

② Is the operational availability at least 75%?

The operational availability of the pacemaker process should be 75% or greater. If not, you should first identify the root causes of the poor availability and solve the problems.

覚えておこう！ Remember!

ペースメーカー工程には、必ずアンドンを！

—異常の見える化は必須！

ペースメーカー工程では、バッチサイズを小さくし、段取り替えを頻繁に行いながら製造することが求められます。この結果、人々は、押し込み生産の時代には気にならなかった小さなトラブル（チョコ停、不良発生、部品異常、作業の遅れ等々）に直面することになります。つまり、押し込み生産の時代に比べて、もっと素早く問題に対処することが必要になるのです。もうわかりましたね？ ペースメーカー工程にはアンドンを必ず付けましょう！

Pacemakers Should Have an Andon!

—Try Andon to Spot Abnormalities

We should pursue smaller batches with more frequent changeover at the pacemaker. Consequently, people will face new problems such as minor stoppages, making defects, defective materials, and delays of operation that might have been regarded as not so big or serious problems when they were producing large batches. That means much quicker corrective actions will be required with heijunka, compared to batch-and-queue production. Try andon at your pacemaker for immediate detection of abnormalities!

アンドンは、現場の状態がステーションごとにひと目でわかるように表示し、また何か異常があればすぐに知らせることができる、目で見る管理の道具です。
ひもスイッチとアンドンを組み合わせることで、素早く問題を発見し、対処することができるようになります。

Andon is a visual management tool to highlight the status of operations in each station at a single glance and to tell you immediately whenever something abnormal occurs.
Employing an andon with a signal cord in assembly operations will enable you to identify problems immediately and to take quick countermeasures.

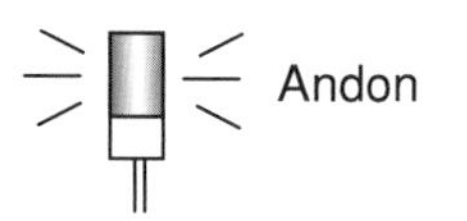

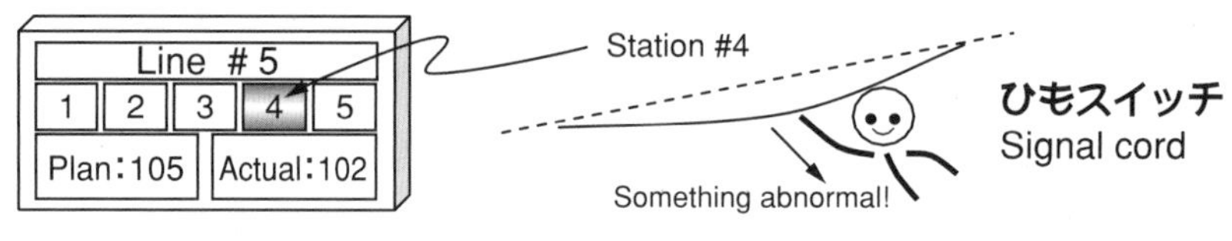

ペースメーカー工程で、量と機種を平準化する
Leveling Quantity and Product-Mix at the Pacemaker

Batch size for each category

Demand per day：1,220 pieces
7.5 hrs/day, 3 shifts/day, Takt Time: 66 sec.

Product category	Number of items	Demand	QTY. per day	Pitch interval	Batch size	EPE
A item	8	60%	720	36	80	1 day
B item	8	20%	240	12	60	2 days
C item	13	20%	260	13	40	2 days
Total	29	100%	1,220	61		

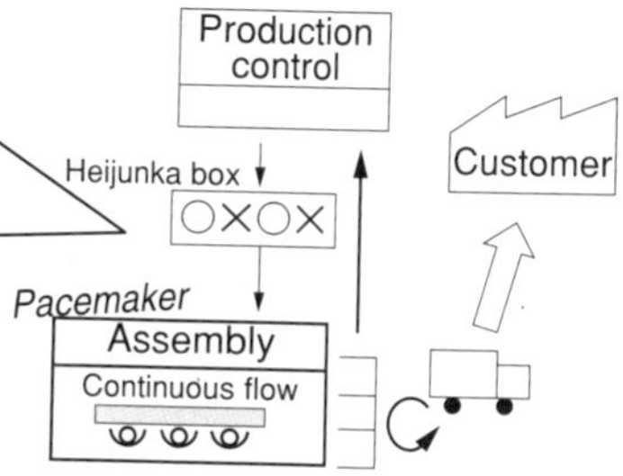

Let's talk ペースメーカーで平準化した生産指示を出す Heijunka at the pacemaker

A: 最終組立ラインの段取り改善の結果、段取り替えが２分以内でできるようになりました。

A: We have improved changeover time in the final assembly line and can now change settings for each item within two minutes.

B: それはすごいよ！ サイクルタイムのバラツキはどのくらいあるの？

B: Good work! Now, how much difference is there in cycle time between items?

A: タクトタイムは66秒、サイクルタイムは最短で56秒、最長で66秒です。ですから、このラインで、この製品群の全機種を平準化して流せますよね。

A: Takt time is 66 seconds. The shortest cycle time is 56 seconds and the longest one is 66 seconds. So, we are going to produce all items for this family on this line, leveling both quantity and product-mix.

B: それで、この差立板をつくったんだね？ 66秒×20個/トレーだから、ピッチは1,320秒、22分か……。これも平準化を始めるのにはちょうどいいね。

B: So, that's why you made this heijunka box? Let's see, multiplying the takt time of 66 seconds by the pack quantity of 20 pieces will show the pitch to be 1,320 seconds, or 22 minutes… So this is a great place to start heijunka.

A: これが機種ごとのバッチサイズです。毎日注文がある機種は毎日つくります。これが８機種あります。そのほかの機種は２日に１回つくります。

A: These are the batch sizes for each item. Each day we will produce the eight items that are ordered every day by the customer. We will produce the other items every two days.

B: 水すましのルートと作業は分析した？

B: Have you analyzed the mizusumashi work content and set the route?

A: はい、15分です。

A: Yes. The route will be 15 minutes.

Chapter

3

自働化と設備改善
Jidoka and Machines

自働化

What Is Jidoka?

にんべんのついた自働化

にんべんのついた自働化は、トヨタ生産方式の2本柱のうちの1つの柱なのですが、ジャスト・イン・タイムに比べて認知度がやや低いかもしれません。しかしながら、これはジャスト・イン・タイムが有名すぎるがゆえに起きていることであって、自働化の重要性がジャスト・イン・タイムに比べて小さいことを意味するものではありません。本書で説明する主な概念と同じように、自働化についても、自動停止やひもスイッチのようなテクニック以前の問題として、佐吉翁の自動織機にそのルーツがあることや、TPSにおける自働化の位置づけといった基本をしっかり学ぶことで、理解をより深めることができます。

私たちは、どの言語でも、TPS用語として日本語の" jidoka" をそのまま使いますが、英語では、"intelligent automation" や "automation with a human touch"、あるいは "autonomous automation" からの造語 "autonomation" を使うこともあります。

自働化の主要な機能は2つです(①異常検知で自動停止する，②警告を発する)。しかし、もうひとつ、大切な意義があるのです。それは、人の仕事と機械の仕事を分けること、そして、機械(ソフトウェアを含むどのような設備や装置でも)が人のために働くのであって、人が機械のために働くのではな

Jidoka or Automation with a Human Touch

Jidoka is, of course, the lesser known of the two pillars of TPS. Just because it is less famous than just-in-time doesn't mean it is any less important. It takes both pillars to support the roof! As with other key concepts introduced in this book, it is helpful to understand the basics of jidoka as it originated in Sakichi Toyoda's automatic loom and the critical necessity of jidoka in TPS before learning the techniques like automatic stopping systems and signaling cords.

We use the Japanese word "jidoka" in any language as a technical TPS term. In English, other terminology that is sometimes used includes "intelligent automation," "automation with a human touch," or "autonomation" (coined from "autonomous automation").

Jidoka has two main features; 1) an automatic stop and 2) an alert. But it also has another key dimension, that of separating human work from machine work and ensuring that machines (or any equipment, including software) work for people, not the other way

いことをはっきりさせることです。異常を検知したら即座に停止し、不良をぜったいにつくらないという、とてもユニークなトヨタの仕事のやり方を、自働化という言葉は如実に表しています。

around. Jidoka refers to the characteristic of work to have the ability to detect any abnormalities and stop itself so as not to produce defects.

自働化とは？
自働化とは、異常発生を検知して即座に停止し、対策をとる機能を、設備と作業者に与えることを意味します。

What is jidoka?
Jidoka means providing equipment and operators the ability to detect when an abnormal situation has occurred and immediately stop work to institute countermeasures.

なぜ自働化が求められるのか？
設備やプロセスが自働化されていなければ、不良を防ぐために、作業者は設備を見張っていなければなりません。自働化によって、各プロセスで品質をつくり込むことができ、人と設備の動きを分けて、よりムダのない働きとすることができるのです。

Why should we adopt jidoka?
Where machines and processes do not equip themselves with jidoka, operators are needed to keep watch on equipment to prevent defects. Jidoka enables operations to build in quality at each process and to separate operators from machines for more efficient work.

「人と機械の仕事を分ける」ことが、なぜ大切なのか？
機械の見張り番から作業者を解放すれば、機械が加工している間に、作業者に付加価値を生む別の仕事をしてもらうことができます。たとえば、機械の多台持ちや多工程持ちです。

What can we achieve through separating human work from machine work?
Freeing operators from simply monitoring machines through jidoka enables operators to do other value-creating work during a machine cycle (for example, multi-machine handling and multi-process handling).

Automation

ji dō ka
自動化

Automation with a Human Touch

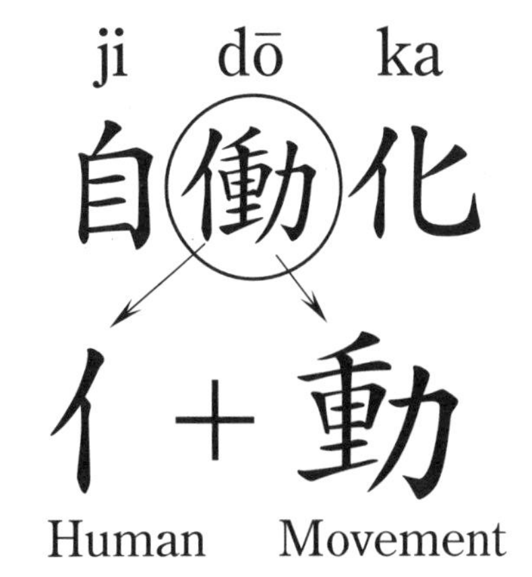

Note: The kanji 働 means "work." It was developed in Japan and is used but not commonly in China. The part 亻 (referred to as nin-ben) means "human" and 動 means "movement." So, human intelligence applied to movement comprises 働 (work).

注：漢字「働」は日本製の漢字で、中国ではあまり使われない。単なる動きに「にんべん＝人の知恵」を付けて、「働き＝はたらき」になる。

にんべんのついた自働化のルーツは、20世紀初頭に発明された佐吉翁の自動織機

Jidoka Originated from the Automatic Loom Invented by Sakichi Toyoda in the Early 20th Century

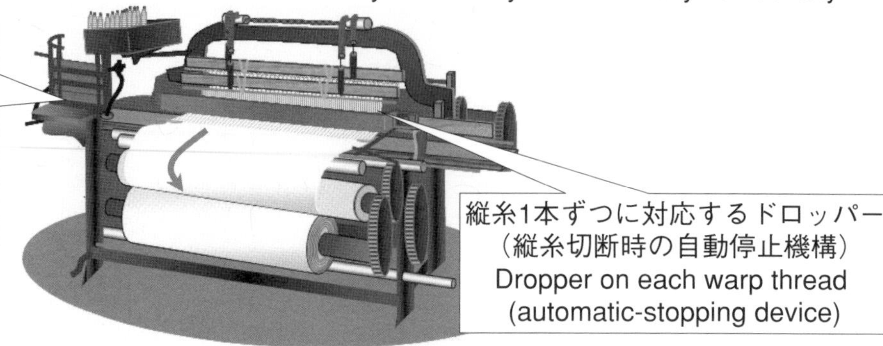

自働化とジャスト・イン・タイムのルーツ
——近代日本の二人の偉人

自働化とジャスト・イン・タイムのルーツは、ともに戦前(第2次世界大戦前)にあります。トヨタグループの社祖である豊田佐吉翁(1867～1930)は、20世紀初頭に自動織機を発明し、後に自働化と呼ばれることになる概念を具現化しました。佐吉翁の子息であり、トヨタ自動車の創業者・豊田喜一郎氏(1894～1952)は、1930年代にジャスト・イン・タイムの概念を提唱しました。

The Roots of Jidoka and Just-in-Time
——Two Great Creators in Modern Japan

Jidoka and just-in-time both have their roots in the pre-World War II period. In the early 20th Century, Sakichi Toyoda (1867–1930), founder of the Toyota Group, realized the concept of jidoka, a key feature of his invention of an automatic loom. Kiichiro Toyoda (1894–1952), son of Sakichi and founder of the Toyota automobile business, developed the concept of just-in-time in the 1930s.

佐吉翁の自動織機

佐吉翁は、経(たて)糸が切れたら自動停止する自動織機を発明しました。この自動織機は、横糸がなくなる直前にシャトル(杼・ひ)を自動排出し、新たなシャトルを自動供給する機構も備えていました。この間も織機はフルスピードで動き続け、止まることはありませんでした。

これによって、品質と生産性において劇的な改善が得られるとともに、織機に張り付くことから作業者を解放し、付加価値を生む別の仕事をしてもらうこともできるようになったのです。

その後、異常が発生したら自動停止し、異常を知らせるように設備を設計するという考え方は、トヨタのあらゆる設備、あらゆるライン、あらゆる仕事のやり方において、不可欠なものとなりました。

The Auto Loom Invented by Sakichi Toyoda

Sakichi Toyoda invented an automatic loom that would stop automatically for problems. He equipped his loom with the ability to stop whenever a warp thread broke and to eject almost-empty shuttles quickly and then insert a new one at the last second before the weft thread in each shuttle was completely consumed, all while the machine was operating at full speed. It enabled great improvement in quality and productivity, freeing operators to do more value-creating work than simply monitoring automatic looms.

Eventually the concept of designing machines to stop automatically and call immediate attention to problems became a critical feature of every machine, every production line, and every Toyota operation.

ワンポイントレッスン One-Point Advice

自働化のステップ

佐吉翁の事跡に学び、まずは加工のプロセスをよく観察することから、自働化へのステップは始まります。この時、人の動きと機械の動きを分けて見ることが大切です。

Levels of Jidoka

The first step of jidoka is to carefully observe the process with an eye to incorporate the concepts of Sakichi Toyoda. It is important to learn to see the movements of humans and machine as separate and distinct motions.

	ロード（ワークを機械へセット） Load	起動 Start	マシンサイクル Machine cycle	停止 Stop		アンロード（ワークの取り出し） Unload
				正常 Normal	異常検知 Abnormal	
1	☺	☺	☺	☺	☺	☺
2	☺	☺	Auto	☺	☺	☺
3	☺	☺	Auto	Auto	☺	☺
4	☺	☺	Auto	Auto	Auto	☺
5	☺	☺	Auto	Auto	Auto	Auto
6	☺	Auto	Auto	Auto	Auto	Auto
7	Auto	Auto	Auto	Auto	Auto	Auto

面対照配置の自動織機が多台持ちを加速した

Mirror-Symmetric Setting of Toyoda Auto Looms Boosted Multi-Machine Handling

豊田式自動織機は面対照の配置が可能でした。これにより、シャトル供給作業と織機の再スタート動作の場所が近接化され、作業者の動作のムダを省き、より多くの多台持ちができるようになったのです。

Sakichi's auto looms were designed to be effective with a mirror-symmetric setting. It made it possible to co-locate the operator's movements when changing shuttles and starting machines, eliminating tremendous amounts of waste of motion and enabling operators to handle many more machines at the same time.

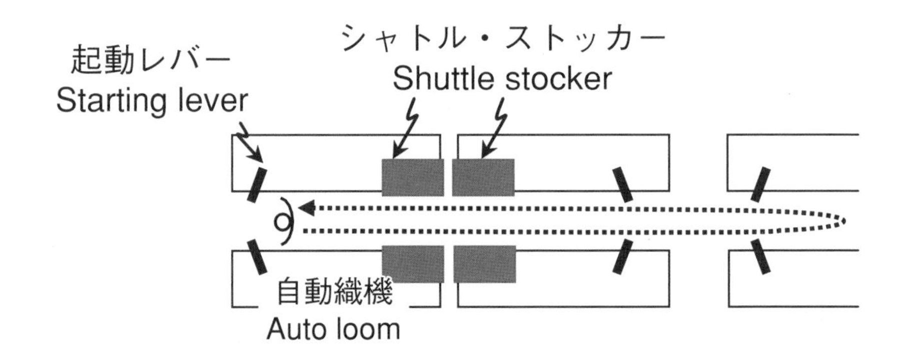

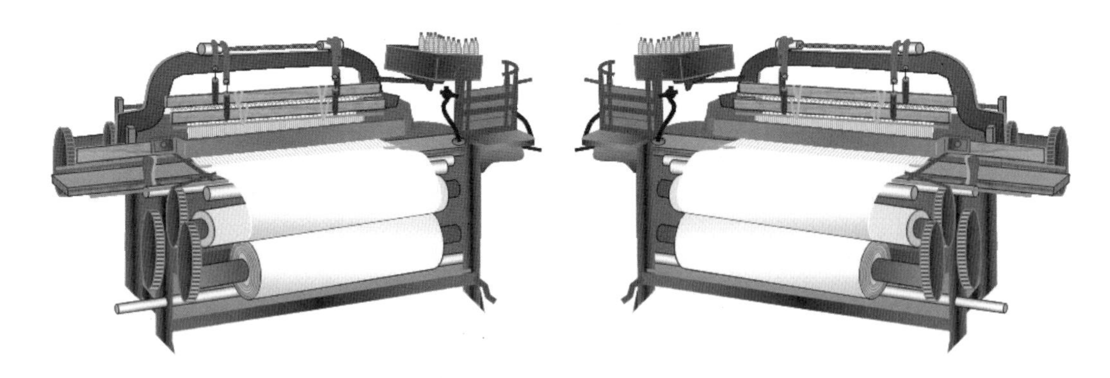

面対称配置　Mirror-Symmetric Placement

あっ、それは、人のムダづかい！
What a Lavish Expenditure of Human Ability!

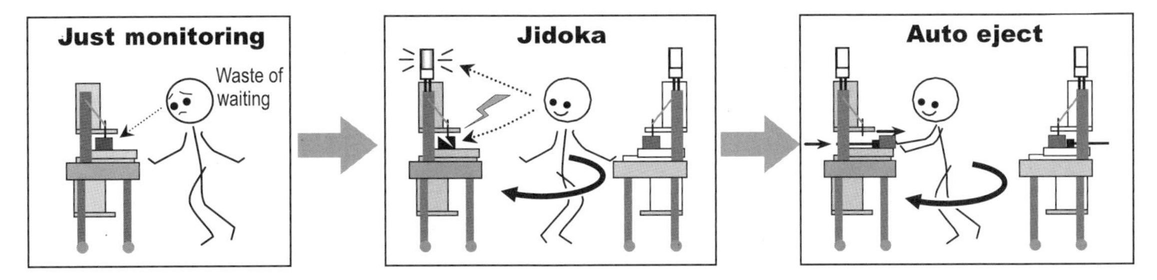

Let's talk もったいないっ !! Mottai-nai!: How wasteful!

A: 組立セルでは、タクトタイムより少しだけ短いサイクルで、安定してつくれるようになったんですよ、ほら。

A: Here, our assembly cell has been improved to operate stably with the cycle time a little shorter than the takt time.

B: あーっ！　もったいないっ！

B: Whoa! Mottai-nai!!

A: モ…モッタイナイ？　それは何？

A: Mo…. Mottah-i-na-i!?　What do you mean?

B: 「もったいない」は、「わぁ、これって、ものすごくムダだよね！」っていうような意味なんだよ。ほら、溶接の作業者は、機械が動いている間、付加価値を付ける動作を何もしてないよね？

B: "Mottai-nai" means "How wasteful!" You see that the operator at the welding process really does nothing value-creating during machine cycle, don't you?

A: その通りなんだけど、仕方がないわ。不良が発生するかもしれないし。それに、部品を取り付けて、取り外す人は必要ですもの。

A: Yes, you are right. But there is no alternative, because the machine might make defects. And someone needs to set parts and pick them up.

B: それは人の能力のムダ遣い。「もったいない」の1つだよ。自働化の話を覚えているかな？

B: This is a lavish expenditure of human ability. This is one Mottai-nai — very wasteful — practice. Do you remember jidoka?

A: あ、ジドウカ、つまり異常があったら自動停止ですね！　教わったことがあります。でも、取付けと取外しがあるから、彼女の手待ちの時間はそんなに長くはないわ。

A: Yes, jidoka—we know about it … But, the loading-and-unloading work does not cause her too much waiting time.

B: そこで、「ハネ出し」の出番なんだ。

B: So now it is time to consider an auto-eject device.

Chapter 3 自働化と設備改善 — 2
Jidoka and Machines

稼働率と可動率

Operating Rate vs. Operational Availability

稼働率と可動率とは？

稼働率は皆さんご存知の通り。可動率とは、TPSの進化と深化の過程で考え出された考え方の１つで、設備やシステムが動いてほしいときに、どのくらい正しく動いているかを示す指標です。稼働率と区別するため、「べきどうりつ」とも読みます。TPMに取り組んでいて、すでにさまざまな設備稼働管理指標を用いている工場で説明する時には、混乱を招かないよう、特に注意すべきでしょう。

What Is Operating Rate? What Is Operational Availability?

While “operating rate” is one of most common metrics to be found in any manufacturing site, “operational availability” (OA) is a unique concept developed during the hard work of evolving TPS. OA is a measure that digs into how effectively the operation works as required. In Japanese, it is also called “bekidō ritsu (可動率 - operational availability)” to distinguish it from common “kadōritsu (稼働率 - operating rate).”
Careful explanation of the terms can be especially important at work sites that have experience with TPM (Total Productive Maintenance) and its various metrics around machine utilization.

稼働率とは？
稼働率とは、ある期間（シフト、日など）に、設備が何かをつくるために使われている時間が、どのくらいあるかを示すものです。

Operating rate
The operating rate means the amount of time in a time frame (shift, day, etc.) that a machine is used to make something.

可動率とは？
可動率とは、設備が必要なときに正しく動く割合です。

Operational availability
The operational availability is the fraction of time that a machine functions properly when needed.

稼働率と可動率 Operating Rate vs. Operational Availability

稼働率 Operating Rate		可動率 Operational Availability
Actual run-time (実際に動いていた時間) / **Available production time** (想定する稼働時間)	**VS.**	**Cycle time* × Required qty.** (必要数に対して決められた所要時間) / **Actual time to produce** (実際にかかった時間)

*Cycle time does not include any failures, adjustments, minor stoppages, or defects in this calculation.

高稼働率のワナ

高い設備稼働率を維持するのは一見よいことのように感じられますが、後工程が必要としているか否かに関係なく設備を動かすのなら、それはつくりすぎのムダを生むことになります。稼働率は、お客様である後工程が求める量に応じて、高くも低くもなるものです。

The trap of chasing high operating rate

Keeping a high operating rate sounds efficient on the surface, but the waste of overproduction results when we run machines without relation to any need of the customer processes downstream. The operating rate may be high or low according to the need of its customers, or the processes downstream.

可動率は100％が理想

高い稼働率は常によいとは言えませんが、可動率は100％が理想です。

The ideal operational availability is 100%

A high operating rate is not necessarily desirable, but the ideal operational availability rate should be 100%.

設備総合効率

設備総合効率は、TPMの重要な指標の1つで、設備がどのくらいムダなく使われているかを示すものです。設備総合効率は、3つの要素の掛け算で計算されます。

時間稼働率×性能稼働率×良品率

Overall Equipment Effectiveness (OEE)

OEE is one of the essential TPM metrics. It measures how effectively equipment is being used and is calculated through the multiplication of three elements:

Availability Rate × Performance Rate × Quality Rate

※上記(右段)英訳語の"Availability Rate"(時間稼働率のTPM英訳語)は、"可動率＝Operational Availability"とイコールではないことに留意して下さい(可動率は、〔時間稼働率×性能稼働率〕の意味で使われたり、OEEとほぼ同じ意味で使われることも多い概念です)。

Note that "availability rate" in the above OEE formula is not always the same as "operational availability." Availability rate is the translation for the Japanese TPM term "時間稼働率 (time-based operating rate)". Because operational availability is a concept, it is sometimes interpreted as having the same meaning as [Availability Rate × Performance Rate] (a part of OEE) and other times is used interchangeably with OEE itself. These misinterpretations can lead to much confusion.

設備の6大ロス …… **The six major losses in machinery**

①故障
②段取り
③チョコ停
④速度ロス
⑤不良
⑥手直し
※上記以外にもさまざまなロスを採用している企業・組織があります。

① Breakdown
② Changeovers and adjustments
③ Minor stoppages
④ Speed losses
⑤ Scrap
⑥ Rework
※Some companies and associations employ additional metrics.

作業者も保全の一翼を担う …… **TPM involves production workers in maintenance activities**

保全担当者による従来の予防保全とは異なり、TPMでは、作業者を巻き込み、日常の保全や改善活動、簡単な修理も作業者が行うことを目指します。たとえば、潤滑油のチェックと補充、清掃、増締め、設備の点検などです。

Unlike traditional PM, which relies on skilled maintenance personnel, TPM involves operators in routine maintenance, kaizen activities, and simple repairs, such as lubricating, cleaning, tightening, and inspecting machines.

覚えておこう！ Remember!

TPS and TPM

TPMのルーツも、トヨタ・グループのデンソーにあった！
TPM originated at Denso, the Toyota Group company

1971年、日本電装*がJIPE**主催のPM賞を受賞します。この時、同社の設備保全に対する優れた全社的な取組みがJIPEの審査員によって注目されました。これがTPMのルーツとされています。それ以前には、PM活動の多くは保全部門のものと考えられていたのです。

In 1971, Nippondenso * was awarded the distinguished plant prize for PM, by JIPE **. The JIPE auditors were impressed with Nippondenso's company-wide PM activities. The origin of "T" PM has been credited to Nippondenso since that time. Until then, most PM activities had been assigned to skilled maintenance personnel.

*日本電装 Nippondenso: Former name of Denso（現・㈱デンソー）
**JIPE: Former name of JIPM（現・㈳日本プラントメンテナンス協会）

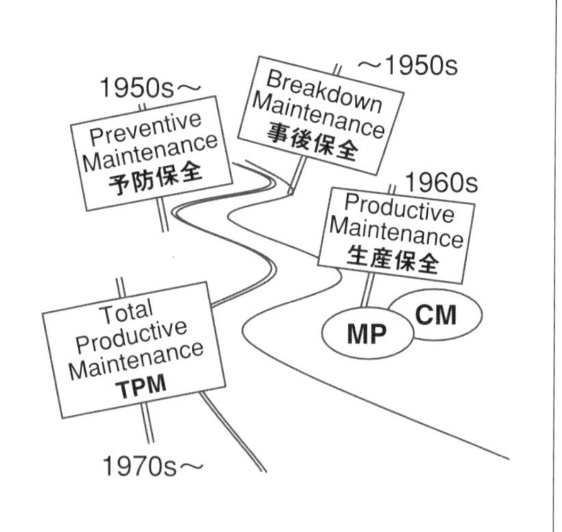

ワンポイントレッスン One-Point Advice

なぜを5回繰り返せ！

「5回のなぜ」とは、問題に出会ったら、常に目に見える現象を超えて、真因に到達するまで「なぜ？」を繰り返すべし、という意味です。

その著作「トヨタ生産方式」(1978、ダイヤモンド社)に書かれた大野耐一氏の「5回のなぜ」を復習しましょう。

1. なぜ機械は止まったか？
   オーバーロードがかかって、ヒューズが切れたからだ。

2. なぜオーバーロードがかかったのか？
   軸受部の潤滑が十分でないからだ。

3. なぜ十分に潤滑しないのか？
   潤滑ポンプが十分にくみ上げていないからだ。

4. なぜ十分くみ上げないのか？
   ポンプの軸が磨耗してガタガタになっているからだ。

5. なぜ磨耗したのか？
   ストレーナー(濾過機)が付いていないので、切粉が入ったからだ。

The Five Whys

The phrase "Five Whys" means the practice of asking why repeatedly whenever a problem is encountered to get beyond the obvious symptoms to identify the root cause.
Let's review the "Five Whys" in *Toyota Production System* written by Taiichi Ohno (1988, NY. Productivity Press).

1. Why did the machine stop?
   There was an overload and the fuse blew.

2. Why was there an overload?
   The bearing was not sufficiently lubricated.

3. Why was it not lubricated?
   The lubrication pump was not pumping sufficiently.

4. Why was it not pumping sufficiently?
   The shaft of the pump was worn and rattling.

5. Why was the shaft worn out?
   There was no strainer attached and metal scraps got in.

チョコ停を改善すれば、リードタイム短縮＆原価低減に加えて、人はもっと活躍できる！
Reducing Minor Stoppages Reduces Lead Time and Cost, and Enables an Operator to Do Additional Work!

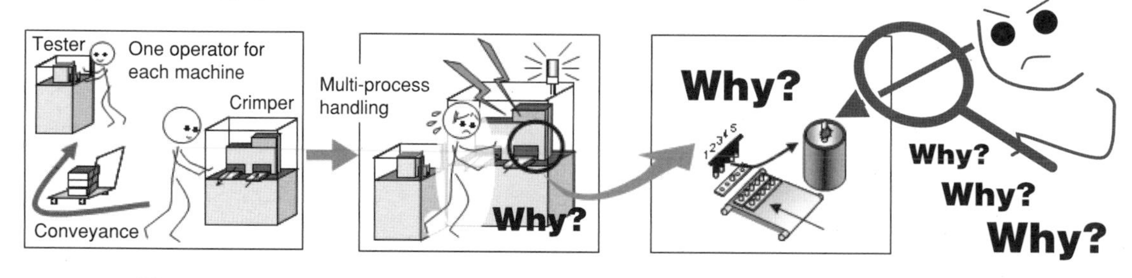

Let's talk 真因に至るまで、現地・現物・現実で追究！ Pursue the true root cause based on your gemba (*genchi, genbutsu,* and *genjitsu*) realities!

A: 金曜日から、カシメ機と検査の多工程持ちを始めましたが、生産量が計画に達しません。

A: We have implemented multi-process handling from crimping to testing since Friday, but the output has not reached the target yet.

B: この２つは、ラインの最終工程だね？　改善を始める場所としてはまあ正しいよね。…でも、カシメ機のチョコ停がどのくらい起きているか、わかってる？　ほら、またまた止まった！　今すぐ、…そうだなあ、最低でも２時間は、工程をよく観察しなくちゃね！

B: Are these two the final processes of this line? This is basically the right place to start. But, do you know how often the crimping machine stops? Now, it has just stopped. And again! You should observe this process starting now for at least ...... two hours!

《…２時間後…》

《…Two hours later…》

A: わかりましたよ！　カシメ機では、１度に５個ずつ加工するのですが、３番目のピッキングアームが部品をしょっちゅう取り損なっていたのです。そこで、３番目のヘッドを交換したら、チョコ停がほとんどなくなりました。

A: We found the problem! It crimps five work pieces at a time. The clue was that the third picking-arm often had missed parts. So I replaced its head with a new one. Since then, almost no minor stoppage has occurred.

B: よかったね。では、３番目のヘッドが部品を取り損なっていたのはどうして？

B: Good! Well, did you get at the reason why the third one had so often missed parts?

A: ヘッドのガイド溝が変形していました。理由はわかりませんが…。

A: Its guide-flute had collapsed. We don't know why ...

B: 真因がわかるまで、「なぜ？」を繰り返さなくちゃいけないよ。

B: You should repeat more "Whys" until you determine the root cause.

自働化と設備改善 — 3
Jidoka and Machines

段取り改善
Setup Reduction

なぜ段取り改善が必要なのか？

段取り時間が長ければ、大バッチでつくらざるを得ません。しかし、お客様(後工程)の必要に応えながら在庫を減らしたいと願うなら、答えは1つ、段取り時間の短縮しかないのです。一般に、下流の組立ラインの段取り改善は比較的短期間のうちに実現可能であり、またぜひそうすべきものですが、上流工程のバッチプロセスでは、技術部門はもちろんのこと、設備メーカーも巻き込んだ粘り強い活動が求められます。期間も長期にわたるでしょう。だからこそ、単に「段取り時間を短縮せよ」と指示するのではなく、段取り時間短縮が平準化生産の実現にとって不可欠であり、トータルリードタイム短縮と在庫削減に必ず結び付くという確信を、関係者全員に持ってもらうことが重要なのです。

Why Setup Reduction?

When changeover times are too long, you have no choice but to produce in large batches. If you want to reduce your inventories while also successfully meeting customer requirements, the key is to shorten changeover times for all operations. Generally speaking, we can shorten changeover times at downstream assembly processes relatively easily and quickly, but setup time reduction at upstream batch-type processes will often demand your tenacious efforts and require the support of engineers and machine suppliers. That is why we have to work very hard to ensure that everyone along such value streams believes firmly that shortening changeover times is essential to achieve **heijunka** production and that **heijunka** will result in shorter lead times and lower inventories. It will not do to simply try to order people to shorten changeover times when they don't understand.

段取りとは？

段取りとは、単体設備や自動化ラインで、1つの型番の製品または部品の生産から、違う型番の製品または部品の生産に切り替えることを言います。部品やプレス金型、モールド金型、治具などを交換して切り替えるのです。

Changeover

Changeover means the process of switching from the production of one product or part number to another in a machine or a series of linked machines by changing parts, dies, molds, fixtures, etc.

段段取り時間とは？

段取り時間とは、最後の１個が完成した後、段取りを行ってから最初の１個目の良品が出てくるまでの時間です。

Changeover time

Changeover time is measured as the time elapsed between the last piece in the run just completed and the first good piece from the process after the changeover.

ロットを小さく、段取り替えを速やかに

バッチプロセスの段取り時間をシングル（10分以内）まで短縮できるのなら、段取り回数を増やすことによって、後補充のリードタイムを大幅に減らすことができるでしょう。

Producing smaller batches with quick changeovers

You will be able to considerably reduce replenishment lead time in batch process with additional changeovers, if changeover times can be taken down to a single digit, or less than 10 minutes.

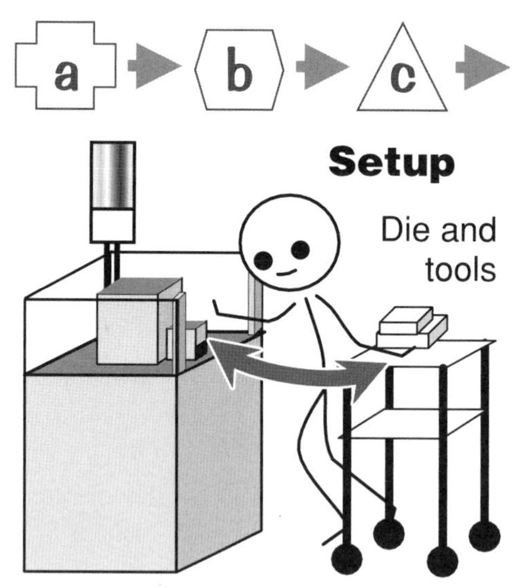

段取り改善の目標をどのように設定するか？

How Should We Set the Targets in Setup Reduction?

「改善はお客様に一番近い最終工程から始める」というセオリー通り、段取り改善もまた最終組立ラインの改善の中に位置付けられ、スタートするはずです。まずは、現在の最終組立ラインの段取り時間を正確に測定することが第1歩。下流の工程は、お客様が指定した入り数の単位で機種を切り替えて製品をつくることができるだけの平準化の能力を獲得しなければなりません。一方、最終組立ラインで改善を始めたばかりの時期でも、上流のバッチプロセスの段取り改善に着手することは大きな意味があります。上流の段取り改善は、下流の工程に比べ、時間もお金もかかる場合が多いからです。

From the principle that kaizen should ordinarily begin with the process closest to the customer, your setup reduction activities should also begin in final assembly and expand upstream from there. Your first task is to carefully study and time the setup operation at final assembly. Downstream operations should attain the **heijunka** ability to produce via alternating items every pack-out quantity. On the other hand, even after you have begun improving setup times at your downstream processes, it may be helpful to quickly begin setup reduction at upstream processes due to the fact that it usually costs more and takes longer there—so go ahead and get an early start!

ペースメーカー工程の段取り改善

Setup reduction at the pacemaker process

ペースメーカー工程において、もしも段取り時間がゼロならば、顧客の入り数（収容数）の単位で1機種ずつ切り替えることが可能です。これは理想です。不可能ではありませんが、すぐに実現するのが難しければ、全機種を1日または2日でつくることを最初の目標にしましょう。できるだけ早く、段取り時間をタクトタイム以下まで短縮しなければなりません。

If the setup time is zero at the pacemaker, you can change over one container by one container in the amount of the pack-out quantity. This is the ideal. It is not impossible, but, in such cases where it is hard to immediately realize, you can set the first-stage target to produce every part every day or every two days. Then, you should shorten changeover times down to less than the takt time as soon as possible.

上流のバッチプロセスの段取り改善

Setup reduction at the upstream batch processes

上流のバッチプロセスでは、最初は、段取り時間を少しずつ短縮することから始めて、次のステップとして半分まで短縮しましょう。さらに、シングル段取り（10分以内）が可能になれば、補充リードタイムを大幅に短縮し、在庫をもっと削減することもできるのです。

In the beginning at upstream processes, you had better start with reducing current setup times minute by minute, and then challenge reducing setup times down to half. Eventually, if you can change over within ten minutes, you will significantly shorten your replenishment lead time and reduce your inventories.

段取り改善の目標　How Do You Set the Targets in Setup Reduction?

上流のバッチプロセス
At the upstream batch processes

1. 段取り時間を、絶えず短縮する
2. 段取り時間を半分にする
3. 段取り時間を10分以内にする

1. Reduce setup time minute by minute
2. Reduce setup time down to half
3. Reduce setup time down to a single digit (or less than 10 minutes)

下流のペースメーカー工程
At the pacemaker process

1. 段取り時間をタクトタイム以下まで改善して、すべての機種を1日または2日でつくる
2. 段取り時間ゼロ

1. Every part every day or 2 days with setup time<takt time
2. Setup time=zero

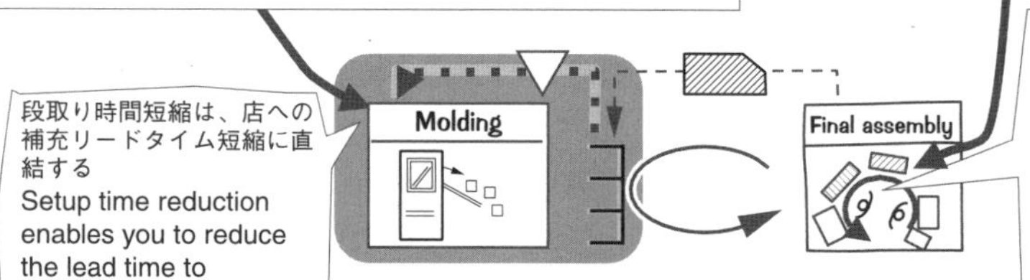

段取り時間短縮は、店への補充リードタイム短縮に直結する
Setup time reduction enables you to reduce the lead time to replenish items in the supermarket.

最終組立ラインでは、入り数単位の平準化の実現を目指すべし。このためには、ペースメーカー工程の段取り時間は限りなくゼロに近いことが求められる。つまり、長くても、
Attain the ultimate *heijunka* ability, which is to change over between each pack-out quantity at the pacemaker process. To do this, changeover times must be reduced to less than the takt time:

段取り時間＜タクトタイム
Changeover time ＜ takt time

ワンポイントレッスン One-Point Advice

段取り改善のステップ

この分野では、特に新郷重夫氏(1909～1990)の研究と実践が日本国内のみならず、北米でもよく知られています。新郷氏は、トヨタの人々とともに現場で研究し、「段取り改善のステップ」として、その考え方と技法を整理しました(参考：「シングル段取への原点的志向」(JMA)1983)

The Basic Steps in Setup Reduction

The studies on setup reduction by Shigeo Shingo (1909–1990) are well-known not only within Japan but also in North America. Shingo studied kaizen with Toyota people at the gemba and then summarized the concept and methods in his book, *A Revolution in Manufacturing: The SMED System* (Productivity Press, 1985; SMED = Single Minute Exchange of Die).

1．現状の段取り時間を測定する。
2．段取り作業を内段取りと外段取りにハッキリ分化し、それぞれの時間を算出する。
3．内段取り要素を可能な限り外段取りに転化する*。
4．外段取り化できずに残った内段取り要素の時間を短縮する。
5．外段取りの時間を短縮する。
6．段取り替えの新手順を、標準化する。

1. Measure the setup time in the current state.
2. Identify the internal and external setup elements, calculating the individual times.
3. Convert as many of the internal elements to external elements as possible.*
4. Reduce the time for the remaining internal elements.
5. Reduce the time for the external elements.
6. Standardize the new procedure.

・内段取り：設備を停止して行う段取り作業

・外段取り：設備を止めなくても行える段取り作業

*新郷氏の提唱のうち、最も特徴的な部分

・Internal Setup Work
Internal setup work can be done only when a machine is stopped.

・External Setup Work
External setup work can be done while a machine is running.

*The most creative and useful of Shingo's ideas

段取り改善の第一歩は、内段取りと外段取りをよく観察して分けること！
Identifying Internal and External Setup Work Is the First Clue to Reducing Changeover Time

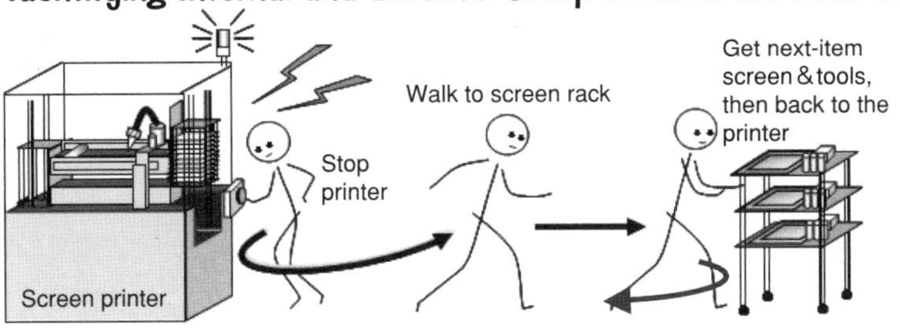

Printer Setup (Current)
1. Stop printer
2. Walk to screen rack
3. Get next screen & tools
4. Walk back to printer
5. Drain remaining graphite
6. Get current-item screen off
7. Set next screen
8. Adjust screen
9. Clean previous screen up
10. Bring screen & tools back to rack

まずは外段取り化！
Convert internal setup work to external!

A: スクリーン印刷工程には、まだ問題が残っています。品目切り替えに約40分かかっているのです。

A: There are problems remaining at the screen-printing process. It takes about 40 minutes to change printing items over.

B: そのおかげで、印刷機の後ろにこんなに在庫を持たなくてはならないんだね。それで、タクトタイムと印刷時間は？

B: So it makes you keep all this inventory next to the screen printer. OK, let me know the takt time and the printing time.

A: タクトタイムは１秒/個、シート１枚50個を一度に印刷します。シート１枚当たりの印刷時間は40秒です。

A: The takt time is one second per piece and 50 pieces on each sheet are printed at a time. The printing cycle time is 40 seconds per sheet.

B: 必要な能力がシフト当たり540シートだよね。540シート印刷するのには360分かかるから、シフト当たり、切り替えに使える時間が90分はある、と。で、これを切り替え時間の40分で割ると…う～ん、シフト当たり２回しか切り替えられないってことか。

B: 540 sheets are required per shift. It takes 360 minutes to produce 540 sheets. Then you have 90 minutes to change the screen over every shift. Dividing 90 minutes by changeover-time 40 minutes, um.., you can currently change the printer over only twice every shift.

A: だから段取り時間短縮が必要なんですよね。まず何をしたらよいでしょう？

A: So we really need to reduce changeover time. What should we do first?

B: まずは、外段取りを分けることだね。ほら、作業者が機械を止めてから、スクリーンと工具を取りに行ったでしょう？

B: First of all, you should separate the external setup elements from the setup work. You can see that the operator is going to get the next item's screen and tools after stopping the printer.

人と機械の仕事を分ける

Separating Human Work and Machine Work

人の能力を最大限に引き出すには？

人は、今の仕事のやり方で見えている能力よりも、ずっと大きな能力を発揮する可能性を秘めています。しかし、現実には、作業者の多くに手待ちがある一方で、ほとんどの工程につくりすぎがあります。人の能力のムダ遣いを減らし、人の能力を最大限に引き出すため、機械から人を離す工夫が必要です。

Making the Most of the Abilities of Our People

People at the gemba always have latent abilities far beyond what is elicited by the current design of operations. Interestingly and disturbingly, while we can often see operators waiting, we can also see overproduction at every process. Some creativity may be necessary to develop and maximize the abilities of everyone, but refuse to relegate anyone to being a wasteful expenditure: free your people from machines!

人と機械の仕事を分けることが第１歩

人と機械の仕事を分けることは、１人ひとりの作業者の能力を最大限に発揮してもらうための第１歩です。

Maximize human ability

Separating human work and machine work is the first step to maximize the abilities of the individual operators.

工程をじっと見る

まず、作業者の手元がよく見える位置に立って、じっと観察しましょう。加工の順序に沿って、人の仕事、機械の仕事を分けて、それぞれの時間を測定します。

Close observation of process

Stand where you can see both operator's hands well and study the process carefully. Separate the operator's work elements and machine cycle according to the process sequence, and then time each of them.

機械から人を離せば、多工程持ちや多台持ちが可能になる！

Freeing Operators from Machines Makes Multi-Process/Machine Handling Possible

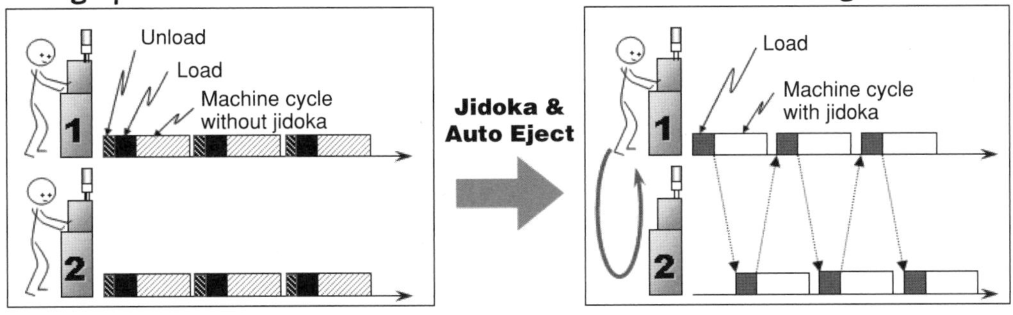

自働化で手待ちをなくす

作業者の手待ちの時間や、単に機械を監視しているだけの時間に着目します。自働化すれば、異常の検知やミスの防止のために人が機械を監視する必要はなくなることに気づくでしょう。

Jidoka to reduce waiting time

Look at waiting and simply-monitoring times. You can understand that operators will have no need to simply monitor machines equipped with jidoka to detect abnormalities and avoid making mistakes.

すべての機械にハネ出しを

それが可能と思えるところならどこにでも、ハネ出しを付けましょう。ハネ出しは、人を機械から離すのに大きな力となるでしょう。

Auto-eject for all machines

You should apply auto-eject everywhere possible. It will greatly help to separate operators from machines.

設備の能力最大化 vs. 人の能力最大化

Maximizing the Utilization of Machines vs. Maximizing the Abilities of Operators

「高い設備稼働率を維持すれば原価が下がる」という伝統的な考え方は、素材産業や上流のバッチプロセス型の現場では、今なお適切と言えるかもしれません。しかし、最終顧客に近づけば近づくほど、設備稼働率の最大化がつくりすぎに直結する危険は増大します。下流のプロセスでは、設備稼働率最大化よりも、人の能力を最大限に引き出すことが求められます。国内・海外を問わず、人離しのテクニック以前の問題として、この考え方をよく理解してもらうことが重要です。

The traditional sense of value that says a high operating rate leads to lower costs may seem suitable to some material industries and some upstream batch-type processes. When we move downstream, closer to the final customers, however, it is easy to see that maximizing the operating rate will result directly in greater and greater overproduction. At downstream processes, maximizing the utilization of people is much more important than maximizing the operating rate of machines. We need to remember this important concept before talking about the specific techniques of separating people from machines.

人、設備、モノのトレードオフ

工程の設計において、人、設備、モノは、トレードオフの関係にあります。3つのうち1つの効率を最大化しようとすると、残り2つの効率は下がってしまいます。

Tradeoffs in people, machines, and materials

There are tradeoffs between people, machines, and materials in designing a process. If you try to maximize one of these three elements, the utilization of the other two will decline.

設備稼働率を最大化すると?

設備稼働率を最大化する、つまりトップスピードで安定して設備を動かそうとするなら、余分な作業者と余分な仕掛りが必要です。

Maximize machine utilization?

Maximizing the utilization of machines or trying to run them constantly at their maximum speed requires extra operators and extra inventory.

モノの効率を最大化(=在庫をゼロに)すると?

モノの効率を最大化するとは在庫ゼロという意味です。在庫をゼロにしようとするなら、需要変動に対応するために余分な作業者と余分な設備が必要です。

Maximize material utilization?

Maximizing the utilization of materials means zero-inventory. If you try to realize this, you will need extra operators and extra machines to meet demand fluctuations.

人の効率を最大化するなら?

おもしろいことに、人の能力を最大化すると、新たな解を得ることも可能です。設備に比べて、人間はとてもフレキシブルだからです。

Maximize operator utilization?

Interestingly, maximizing the utilization of operators can lead you to some new solutions, because humans are much more flexible than machines.

ワンポイントレッスン One-Point Advice

人離しの切り札、ハネ出し！

Auto-Eject, as Leverage to Separate People from Machines

ハネ出しとは、ワークの自動排出機構を設備に付けること。これは、人を機械から離すために欠かせないテクニックです。ワークを排出するのは取り付ける機構よりも安く実現できることが多く、これもハネ出しの特長です。

Auto-eject is a technique to equip a machine with an automatic unloading device. Auto-eject is crucial to free operators from simply waiting until the end of machine cycles. It is highly useful in that you can equip various machines with auto-eject devices at relatively lower costs than loading devices.

ハネ出しと人の動き Operator' s Movement Before/After Auto-Eject

	Procedure (assuming both hands handling)	**Operator's Movement**	
		Before Auto-Eject	**With Auto-Eject**
1	Bring a new work piece to the machine. 新しいワークを設備まで運ぶ	☺	☺
2	Lay it down temporarily near the machine. 持ってきたワークを設備の近くに一時的に置く	☹	—
3	Pick a finished work piece up and lay it down. 完成品を設備から取り出し、一時的に取り置く	☹	—
4	Pick up the new work piece. 新しいワークを取る	☹	—
5	Set the new work piece into the machine. 新しいワークを設備にセットする	☺	☺
6	Push the start-button of the machine. 設備のスタートボタンを押す	☺	☺
7	Machine cycle マシンサイクル	—	—
8	Pick up the finished work piece from the temporary place and bring it to the next process. 完成品を一時的な置き場から取り、次工程へ運ぶ	☺	☺

※ 上の表は両手でなければ持てないワークを想定したもの。2~4項のムダが特に目立つ。
※ Assuming both-hands work, the double-handling in above procedures #2-4 are easy to spot.

人離し、ここにも注目！

Many Things Can Tie People to Machines

せっかくハネ出しを付けたのに、人を離せない。そんなことはありませんか？　次のような点にも目を向けましょう。

- ✓ 起動スイッチや操作ボタンをずっと押し続けなければならない（プレス機など）
- ✓ マシンサイクルの途中で人が機械を操作しなければならない

Auto-eject alone will not usually be enough to completely free operators from machines. Other problems to be overcome include:

- ✓ The operator has to continually press a start or run button to operate the machine (some presses and other machines)
- ✓ The operator has to intervene during the machine cycle

覚えておこう！ Remember!

チャクチャクとは？

ハネ出しを説明したら、チャクチャクについても言及したくなるのが人情というもの。しかし、英語での定番表現は存在しないようです。日本語のチャクチャクをそのまま使って、"Chaku-chaku means 'load-load' in Japanese"。本物のラインで、チャクチャク動作をシミュレーションしてみるのも、理解を深めるのに役立つでしょう。

What Is Chaku-Chaku?

In relation to the auto-eject technique, you may want to introduce "chaku-chaku." "Chaku" means "to load" or "loading" and "consistently take hold" in Japanese. So it means something like "load-load" or "loading after loading." You will probably find it easiest to explain "chaku-chaku" by simulating it in your work cell or a mockup.

ハネ出しのイジェクト・アームが完成したワークを自動的に押し出す。不良は決して排出されない。

Eject arm automatically pushes a finished good work piece to eject. Any defects are not to be ejected.

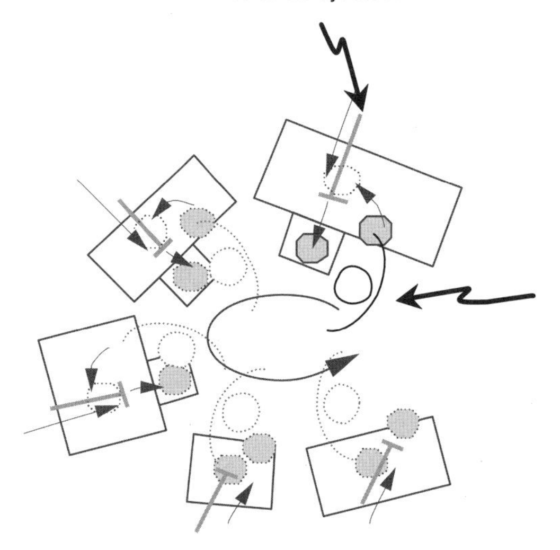

作業者は完成したワークを機械から取り出す必要はなく、ロードだけを繰り返す。（チャクチャクとは、この様子の擬態表現）

Operator does not have to remove finished work pieces from machine. He/she needs simply to load after loading. The term "chaku-chaku" is a mimetic expression of this movement.

ハネ出しは手段、目的は？ Our Goal Is Maximizing the Abilities of People!

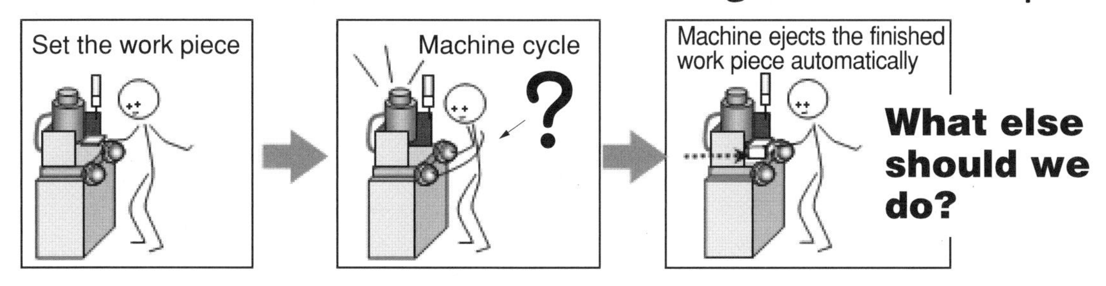

Let's talk 目的は、機械から人を離すこと！ Free operators from machines!

A: ハネ出しのコンセプトをフォーミング機に適用しました。

A: We have applied the auto-eject concept to the forming machine.

B: なるほどね…。う〜ん、惜しいなあ。ほら、彼女、フォーミングサイクルの間ずっと、両手で起動ボタンを押し続けなくちゃいけないっていう問題が、残ったままだよ。

B: That's good. But there is the remaining problem that she has to keep pushing two start-buttons with both left and right hands during the entire forming cycle.

A: しかし、両手スイッチは安全基準ですから、変えるのはちょっと…。

A: But this is our safety standard, so it is hard to change.

B: このままでは、ハネ出しを活かすことができないよ。彼女を機械から解放しなくちゃ。安全のためならエリアセンサやシャッターを使って、起動はリミットスイッチにしてはどう？

B: But in this way, we cannot get the potential efficiency from auto-eject. The objective is to free her from the machine. You can choose infrared sensors or mechanical shutters for protection. Then, how about a limit switch instead of two buttons?

A: あっ！　ハネ出しだけでは不十分なんですね。作業者を機械から完全に離し切らなくちゃいけないんだ！

A: I see. Auto-eject alone is not enough. We must completely free the operator from the machine!

B: そうなんだ、これって、かなりの経験者でも、間違ってしまうことがあるんだよね。それで、両手スイッチをやめたら、彼女は、何秒空くのかな？

B: That's right! This is a common mistake even for experienced people. Anyway, how many seconds will she have, if you get rid of those both-hands buttons?

Chapter 4

工程の安定化
Process Stability

自工程品質保証

What Is Zone Control?

後工程が引き取るモノは「不良ゼロ」でなければならない

ジャスト・イン・タイムは、引き取る部品の中に不良が含まれているようでは、うまく動きません。ストア（店）に置かれた部品や仕掛品は「不良ゼロ」でなければならないのです。

不良品を後工程へ送らないのはかんばんのルール

かんばんのルールのうち５番目は、「不良品を絶対に後工程へ送らない」ということです。

自働化

自働化とは、問題や不良が発生したらいつでもただちに生産が自動的に止まるという意味です。（自働化という言葉が生まれる以前のことですが）豊田佐吉翁が1920年代に発明した自動織機は、自働化を具現化した最初の機械でした。

自工程品質保証とは

マネジメントの階層ごとに、彼または彼女の担当範囲（ゾーン）について深く考察することが推奨されます。理想の世界では、不良を決してつくらないことも可能かもしれませんが、不幸なことに、現実世界では、不良はいつでもどこでも発生する可能性があるものです。しかし、もし不良をつくってしまっても、それを次工程へ送らないようにすることはできます。これを、私たちは「自工程品質保証」と呼びます。自動停止機構は、これらの手法の１つでもあります。

A Pull System Requires "Zero Defects"!

Just-in-time will never work well if defects are hidden in the supermarkets from which customer processes withdraw items. “Zero defects” of all work-in-process (WIP) and parts in every supermarket is necessary.

The fifth of the six rules for kanban

The fifth of the six rules for using kanban effectively is that defective parts are never sent to the next process.

Let’s review jidoka!

Jidoka means ensuring that a production process stops automatically and immediately whenever a problem or defect occurs. The earliest style of jidoka was invented by Sakichi Toyoda in the form of his automatic looms in the 1920s.

What is zone control?

Each management level should think of managing in terms of his or her “zone.” In an ideal world, it might be possible to produce with no defects, but unfortunately accidental defects can occur anywhere at any time in the real world. However, even if we might make defects, we can stop them before they go to the next process. We call this “zone control.” As an example, automatic line stop is one of the methods for zone control.

伝統的な検査による品質保証と、自工程品質保証
Traditional Inspection vs. Lean Zone Control

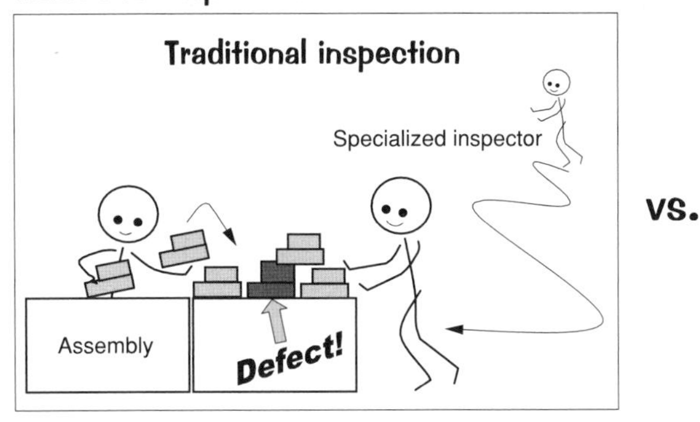

vs.

伝統的な検査による品質保証 ······ Traditional inspection

伝統的な大量生産方式では、ものをつくっている工程とは違う部門に所属する専任の検査担当者が、品質のチェックを行ってきました。

In traditional mass production, a specialized inspector outside of the production process checks for quality.

リーンな自工程品質保証 ······ Lean zone control

リーンなモノづくりでは、つくったところですぐに問題を発見するために、製造工程の作業者に品質保証の権能を持たせ、工程内にポカヨケを付けます。

Lean producers assign quality assurance to operators and employ error-proofing devices within each production process to detect the problems at the sources.

ポカヨケとは? ······ What is "poka-yoke" or error-proofing?

ポカはうっかりミス、ヨケは防止の意味。作業者が間違った部品を取り付けてしまったり、部品を取り付け忘れたり、逆向きに取り付けてしまう等々のミスを犯さないようにするための、シンプルで安価な機構のことです。

"Poka" means inadvertent error, and "yoke" means prevention. Poka-yoke means implementing simple and inexpensive devices that help operators avoid mistakes in their work caused by the wrong parts, leaving out a part, installing a part backwards, etc.

ポカヨケのタイプ ······ The types of error-proofing

- 停止系:最も強力なポカヨケ。例えば、ワークが定位置に正しくセットされなければ始動しない。
- 警告系:ブザー(音)やライト(光)で何か異常があることを知らせるもの。

- Shutdown: These are the most powerful error-proofing devices. For example, a machine will not start if a work piece is set incorrectly.
- Warning: These alert us to something abnormal by a buzzer or light.

ポカヨケのポイント ······ A good error-proofing:

- シンプル、丈夫で長持ちする
- 高信頼性
- 安価
- 現場にマッチしている

- Is simple, with long life and low maintenance
- Has high reliability
- Is inexpensive
- Is designed for the workplace situation

ワンポイントレッスン One-Point Advice

定位置停止

トヨタの最終組立ラインで工夫されてきた「定位置停止」は、異常を検知したらその場で即座に停止するのではなく、決められた1サイクルの仕事が完了する位置までコンベヤが動いた後に停止する仕組みです。異常を検知してから定位置まで動く間に、問題を解決して復旧するのが一番ですが、それができない時は、コンベヤは定位置で停止し、次のサイクルが始まることはありません。

サイクル内の任意の場所で停止すると、問題工程以外の工程で部品の取付けミスなどを誘発する恐れがあります。1サイクル完了まで動いてから停止するのなら、ほかの工程へ品質上・安全上の悪影響を及ぼすことはありません。また、この方法によるのなら、問題があったら停止するという原理を大切にしつつも、停止時間を極小化することが可能になるでしょう。

Fixed-Position Stop System

The fixed-position stop system that Toyota uses in its final-assembly lines is very famous and very effective. Whenever an operator encounters any problem, he or she pulls a rope, which will cause the production line to stop, not immediately, but after the product reaches a predetermined position. Efforts are made to bring the line back into normal operation by solving the problem immediately, but if the problem stays unsolved within the cycle, the conveyor stops at the fixed position.

If the operation having a problem could stop at any position, the work of every other operation would be interrupted, which might cause operator error, such as incorrect assembly. Instead, stopping at the fixed position (i.e., the end of each workstation) will not negatively affect other workstation operations in safety and quality. With this method, stoppage time is minimized yet the jidoka concept is maintained because abnormalities are remedied and defects never passed on.

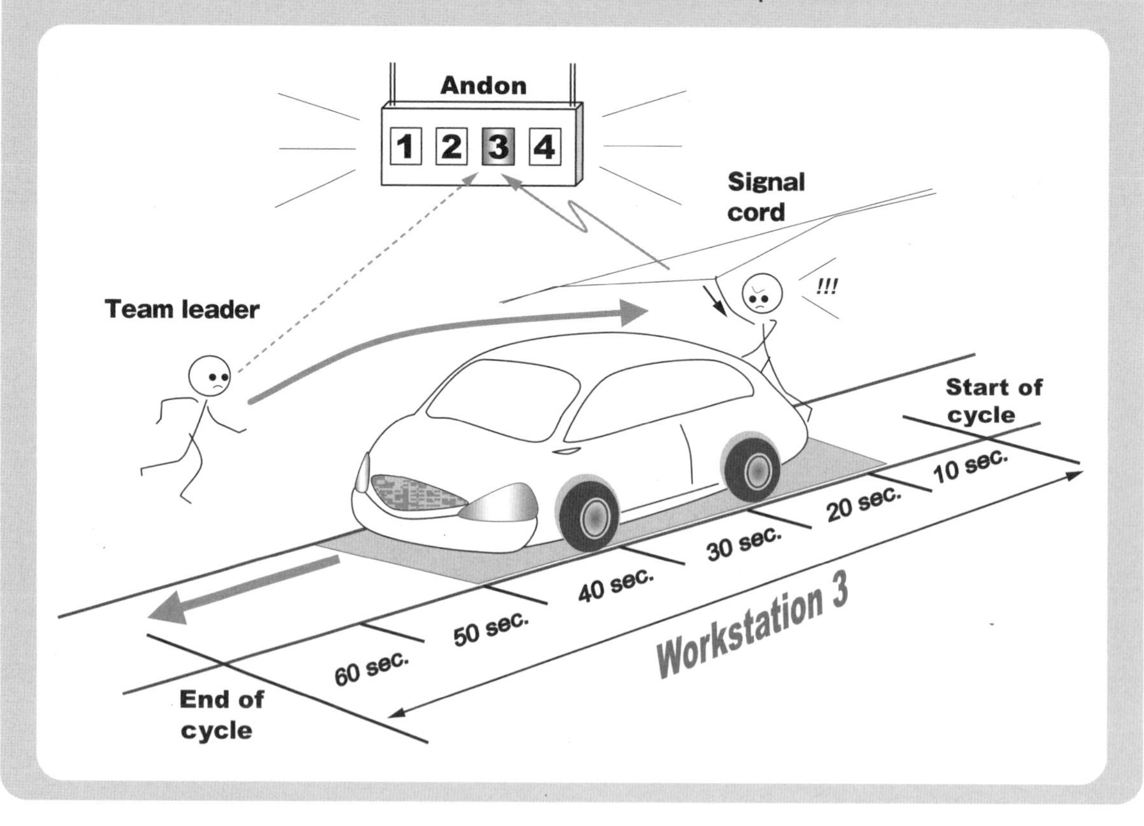

穴あけ工程のポカヨケ　Error-Proofing for the Number of Holes

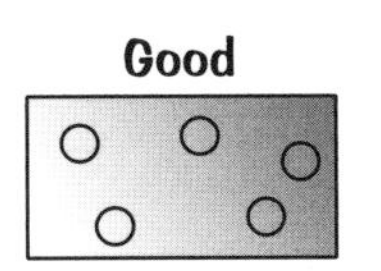

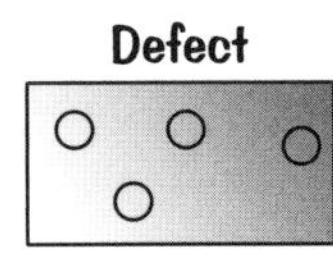

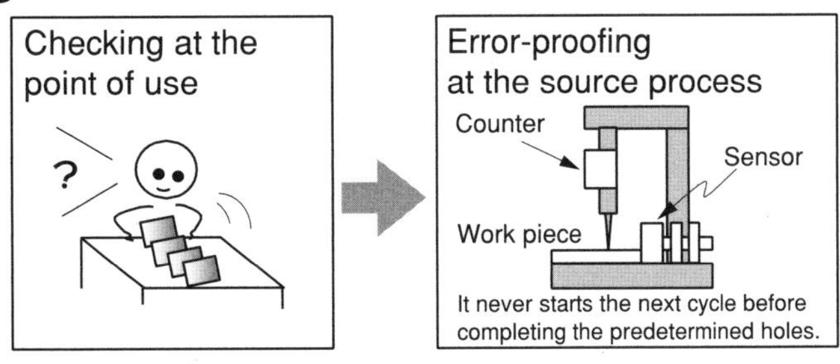

Let's talk カウンターを使って加工数をチェックする Using a counter to control operations

A: 今月は新製品を出しました。既存ラインでつくっています。

A: We launched a new product this month. We produce them with the current production resources.

B: 出来高がばらついているね。それに、総作業量に対して作業者が多くないかな？

B: The output of this line is fluctuating. And don't you have too many operators for the total work content?

A: この金属板の穴の数をチェックするために、作業者を追加する必要がありました。穴あけ漏れは５％で、まだ改善できていません。穴あけ点数不良のために、出来高もばらついてしまうのです。

A: We needed an additional operator to check the number of holes on this metal sheet. The rate of lack of holes is 5% and we have not improved it yet. This causes fluctuation of the output.

B: 使うところでチェックしていたら不良は減らない。源流、つまり穴あけ工程で不良をつくらせないようにした方が効果的だよ。

B: The defects cannot be reduced when you check them at the point of use. It is more effective to prevent operators from making defects at the source process, or the drilling.

A: 決められた数の穴を必ず加工するようにするには――穴あけ機にカウンターを付けるとよいかしら？

A: To drill the holes in the correct number... we can attach a counter to the drilling machine, can't we?

B: よいアイデアだね。生産技術がカウンターやセンサを持っていると思うよ。彼らに、ちょっと来てもらうことはできるかな？

B: That's a nice idea. Production Engineering might have the counters or sensors that you need. Could you ask them to come here now?

標準作業

What Is Standardized Work?

トヨタ生産方式では、どのような業務においても、それが2回以上行われるのなら標準化すべきと、強く推奨されます。作業標準と標準作業の違いがわかるように説明することが大切です。

In the Toyota Production System, any operation that is performed repetitively, even more than once, should be standardized. We should begin by clarifying the difference between standardized work and traditional operation standards.

標準作業とは？

標準作業とは、現在の技術や製法を前提として、良い品質のものを、安全に、より安く、ムダなくつくるための作業の基準です。

What is standardized work?

Standardized work is the basis of operations to make correct products in the safest, easiest, and most effective way based on the current technologies and formulas.

標準作業の3要素

標準作業とは、製造工程の作業者1人ひとりについて、標準作業の3要素に基づく正しい作業方法を定め、定着させることです。

1. タクトタイム
2. 作業順序
3. 標準手持ち

Three elements of standardized work

Standardized work means establishing precise procedures for each operator's work, based on three elements:

1. Takt time
2. Work sequence
3. Standard inventory (In-process stock)

繰返し作業であること

標準作業の作業要素は繰返し作業になっていなければいけません。サイクル外の作業は、流れ化を台なしにし、タクトタイムに合わせてムダなく安定してつくり続けることを不可能にしてしまうものです。これらは必要なものかもしれませんが、チームリーダーや水すましのようなサポートスタッフに担わせるべきです。

Out-of-cycle work

All work elements should be in cycle. Any out-of-cycle work destroys continuous flow and makes it difficult to maintain efficient and consistent production to takt time. These tasks may be needed, but they should be given to supporting members, such as team leaders or mizusumashi (material handlers).

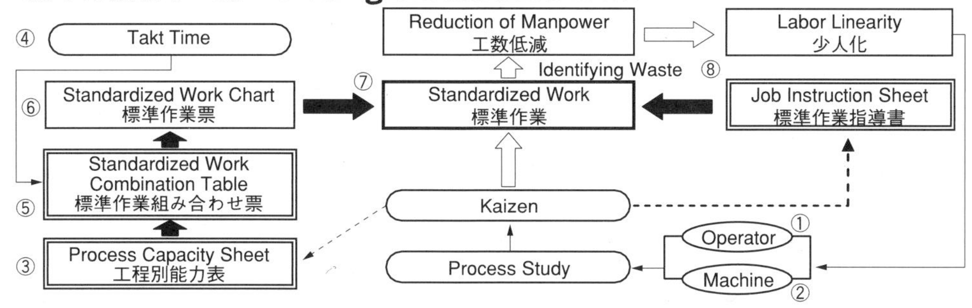

標準作業は何のため？

The Purpose of Standardized Work

改善に唯一最善の解というものは存在しません。管理監督者には、そこに働く人々の人間性を尊重し、ともに作業を設計すること、また現場改善を通して標準作業を継続的に改訂し続けることが求められます。

There is no ultimate solution in kaizen. Leaders should always try to respect their team members as humans, to design the work with them, and to continuously revise their standardized work through kaizen at their workplaces.

標準作業の目的は、継続的な改善の基盤をつくることにあります。これは、それぞれのシフトにおける今の作業のやり方を紙の上に描き出すことであり（表準作業）、作業のバラツキを減らすことになるはずです。また標準作業があれば、新人のトレーニングもやりやすく、ケガや過重な負荷を減らすことにもつながるでしょう。

The purpose of standardized work is to provide a basis for continuous improvement through kaizen. The benefits of standardized work include documentation of current processes for all shifts, reductions in variability, easier training of new operators, and reductions in injuries and strain.

標準作業のつくり方

How to Create Standardized Work

1)工程別能力表 ……………… **1) Process Capacity Sheet**

工程別能力表は、真の加工能力を確定し、ボトルネックを見つけてこれを改善するために、一連の加工工程における機械の能力を計算するために使います。

This is used to calculate the capacity of each machine in a set of processes to confirm true capacity and to identify and eliminate bottlenecks.

2)標準作業組み合わせ票 ……………… **2) Standardized Work Combination Table**

標準作業組み合わせ票は、人の作業と歩行、機械の加工時間の組み合わせを、作業者ごとに順番に書き下すために使うものです。

This is used to describe the combination of manual work time, walk time, and machine processing time for each operator in a sequence.

3)標準作業票 ……………… **3) Standardized Work Chart**

標準作業票は、設備と工程全体のレイアウトと関連付けて、作業者の動きとモノの配置を示すものです。

This shows operator movement and material location in relation to the machine and overall process layout.

4)標準作業指導書 ……………… **4) Job Instruction Sheet**

ワンポイントレッスン One-Point Advice

Process Study

ステップ1：まず、作業を要素に分解する

さて、作業分析です。しかし、いきなりストップウォッチで測ってはいけません。時間測定の前に、まず、1個をつくるのに本当に必要な作業とは何かをよく観察し、作業要素に分解します。作業を要素ごとに分解して観察し、測定することによってムダがよく見え、「廃除」できるようにもなるのです。

Step 1: Dividing the work into the work elements

First, we conduct a process study. Do not begin your process study by first timing the elements with a stop watch. Before timing, observe and list the work elements required to produce one item. Dividing the work into the elements first and then studying them is a helpful way to identify and eliminate waste.

Example of Process Study

Process Study	Process: Tube Assembly for Part#11230			Observer: *Nina Lee*	Page 1/1
Process Steps	OPERATOR			Machine Cycle Time	Notes
	Work Element	Observed Times	Lowest Repeatable		
Assembly 1	*Get tube & press into fixture*				
	Get connector				
	Get hose & place to fixture				
	Push button to start machine				
	Unclamp & remove				
	Place tube				
Assembly 2	*Get tube & fastener*				
	Place to fixture				
	Clamp				
	Place into machine				
	Push button to start machine				
	Remove				
	Unclamp				
	Place tube				

As a work element for future-state work contents, do not include any movement such as below:
下記のような動作は、将来の改善後の作業では、要素として含めてはいけません（廃除されるべきです）。

- ✓ Walking（歩行）
- ✓ Out-of-cycle work（繰返しサイクル外の作業）
- ✓ Waiting for machines to cycle（機械の完了待ち）
- ✓ Waiting for required parts or work pieces（部品待ち）
- ✓ Removing finished parts from machines wherever you believe some auto-eject could be possible
（ハネ出しが可能な場所でのワークの取り出し動作）

ステップ2：作業時間を正しく測定し、個々の作業要素について本当に必要な時間を知る

- 現場で実際の時間を測定せよ。
- 作業者の手の動きがよく見える位置に立て。
- 作業要素ごとに測定せよ。
- それぞれの作業要素を、複数サイクルにわたって何度も測定せよ。
- 認定を得ている作業者を観察せよ。
- 人の時間と機械の時間を常に分けて扱うべし。
- それぞれの作業要素について、測定値の中で、最も速くかつ再現性のある時間を採用せよ(平均値ではなく)。
- 現場での礼儀を忘れるな。

Step 2: Observing and defining the actual time required for each individual work element

- Collect real times at the process.
- Position yourself so you can see the operator's hand motions.
- Time each work element separately.
- Time several cycles of each work element.
- Observe an operator who is qualified to perform the job.
- Always separate operator time and machine time.
- Select the lowest repeatable time for each element (rather than an average time).
- Remember shop floor courtesy.

Note: See the Lean Enterprise Institute workbook *Creating Continuous Flow.*

タクトタイムに合わせるのに必要な作業者は何人？
How Many Operators Do You Need to Meet Takt Time?

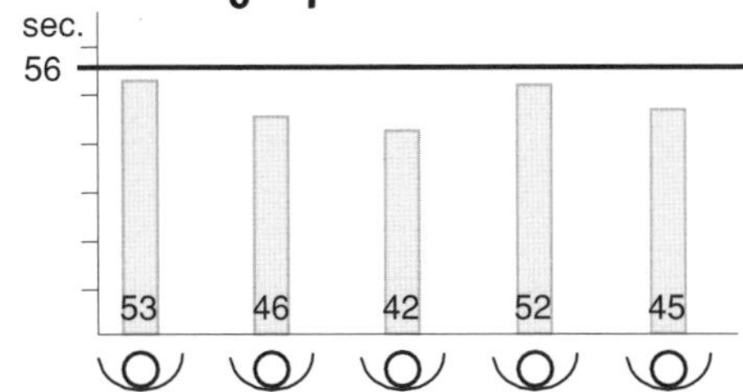

$$\text{The number of operators (作業者数)} = \frac{\text{Total work contents（総作業時間）}}{\text{Takt time（タクトタイム）}} = \frac{238\ \text{sec.}}{56\ \text{sec.}} = 4.25$$

Four operators are not sufficient, but five are too many.

Let's talk 必要な作業者は何人？ How many operators do you need?

A: 前回の改善セッションで、すべての作業者の作業量をタクトタイム以下にすることができました。タクトタイム56秒に合わせて、出来高も安定しています。

A: At the last kaizen session, we made the work contents for each operator less than the takt time. And the output is stable in accordance with the takt time, 56 seconds.

B: 総作業時間は238秒、今の作業者は５人だね。238秒をタクトタイムで割ると、必要な作業者数がわかるんだよ。

B: It takes 238 seconds for the total work contents and you have 5 operators now. Dividing 238 seconds by takt time, you can get the number of operators required here.

A: 4.25人必要ということですよね？ ５人では多過ぎる？

A: You mean that we need 4.25 operators, don't you? And 5 operators are too many?

B: 一般的な話だけれど、この計算結果の端数が0.3未満なら、人を増やすべきではないんだよ。

B: Generally speaking, when the fraction of this calculation is less than 0.3, you should not add one more operator.

A: 各シフトで約30分、残業しなければならないわ。

A: In this case, we will need about 30 minutes of overtime work every shift.

B: 残業できない作業者の分は、君たちリーダーが埋めるんだ。そうしたら、もっと改善しなくちゃいけないって、切実にわかるだろう？

B: You, the team leaders, will have to fill in for the operators who cannot do overtime. You will become aware of the necessity to do much more kaizen, won't you?

A: わかりました。やってみます。

A: Yes, we can do it!

目で見る管理

Visual Management —How to Manage Visually

目で見る管理は改善の基盤

「目で見る管理」は、改善の重要な基盤であり、常に次のステージを目指して継続的に進化すべきものです。日本でも海外でも今や説明不要と思われるほどですが、具体的な手法に注目するあまり、なぜそれが必要なのかという理由の説明を忘れてしまいがちです。注意しましょう。

Visual Management is a Basis of Kaizen

Visual management (VM) is an essential foundation of kaizen and should itself be continuously improved. Visual management is now a very famous lean tool in Japan and other countries, but it is important to explain carefully the purpose and methods of VM. It is easy and common to forget to explain the purpose of VM while focusing intensely on the methods.

目で見る管理とは？

目で見る管理とは、あらゆる治工具や部品、製造の動き、出来高や生産性を、わかりやすく表示することを意味します。こうすれば、関係する誰にでも、製造の状態がひと目でわかるようになります。

What is visual management?

It means the placement in plain view of all tools, parts, production activities, and indicators of production system performance. Then the status of the system can be understood at a glance by everyone involved.

標準なくして管理なし

目で見る管理を私たちの現場で実現するには、まずわかりやすい標準を持たなければなりません。トヨタ生産方式では、標準とは、書棚の分厚い書類のことではありません。標準とは、かくあるべしという姿の、はっきりしたイメージです。

Standards are the basis of visual management

To achieve visual worksite management, start with setting easy-to-understand standards. In the Toyota Production System, “standards” does not mean thick files sitting on a shelf. A standard should be a clear image of a desired condition.

なぜ標準が大切なのか？
標準があるから異常がすぐにわかり、その対策をとることもできるのです。トヨタ生産方式においては、標準とは行動と結び付いたものでなければなりません。

Why are standards so important?
Standards make abnormalities immediately obvious so that corrective action can be taken. In the Toyota Production System, standards should be linked to action.

よい標準とは？
シンプルで明確、視覚的であるべきです。また、標準は常に改善され続けなければなりません。

What makes a standard effective?
A good standard is simple, clear, and visual. And it is always improved.

まずは目で見る管理の基本

Basic Items to Make Visual at the Workplace

それでは、現場で見えるようにすべきものとは、何でしょう？　「すべてが見える」のが理想ですが、まずは最低限、次の項目は必須です。これらが見えるようになっていないなら、すぐに表示しましょう。

What kinds of things should be made visual at the workplace? "Everything visible" is ideal, but begin with the following items at a minimum. Find a way to make these things visible NOW!

①ここはどこ？
ここがどこなのか、誰でもわかるように、製造ラインやストアの所番地と名前を表示します。

① The location address and name
The name and address of each production line (or store) should be displayed clearly so everyone knows where he or she is.

Basic Items to Be Made Visual at the Workplace

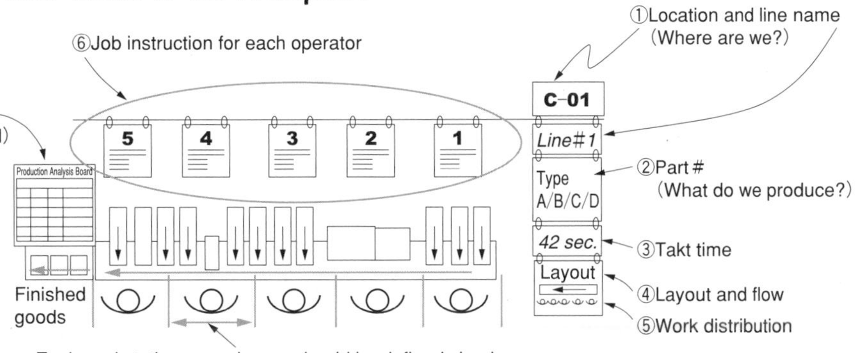

②何をつくっているのか？　何を置いているのか？

製造ラインであれば、何をつくっているのかわかるように表示します。ストアであれば、何を置く場所かがわかるように表示します。
例えば、
- 品番A～Dの組立
- 成形完了部品

② Assigned products/stored materials

In a production line, the name of products produced should be displayed. In a supermarket, the type of materials stored should be displayed. For example:
- Assembly of Parts A, B, C, and D
- Store: Molded Parts

③タクトタイム

顧客が求めるペース。定時稼働時間を顧客要求数で割ったもの。

③ Takt time

The pace required by the customer; the available production time divided by the customer demand.

④レイアウトとモノの流れ ······ **④ Layout and flow of operators, machines, and materials**

⑤作業者の編成 ······ **⑤ Work distribution**

⑥作業内容の指示 ······ **⑥ Job instruction**

⑦計画と出来高（生産管理板） ······ **⑦ Planned vs. actual output (Production Analysis Board)**

計画と出来高は、時間単位でわかるようにしましょう。日次では、生産をうまくコントロールするには不十分です。

Planned versus actual production output should be made visual on an hourly basis. A daily-basis indication is inadequate to control production effectively.

覚えておこう！ Remember!

まず入り数（収容数）を決めよう！

Defining Pack-Out Quantity is the First Step to Parts Visualization

*部品の見える化*の第１歩は、各部品の入り数（収容数）を決めることから始まります。最終製品の入り数の倍数または約数とするのがよいでしょう。「数える」作業を大幅に減らすことができ、正しい数量が保たれているか、トレーの数でわかるようになります。

The first step to *parts visualization* is to define the pack-out quantity of every part. In-process pack-out quantities should be either multiples or divisors of the finished goods pack-out quantity. It can dramatically reduce wasteful "counting" work and you will be able to see at a glance whether parts are maintained within the right quantities or not.

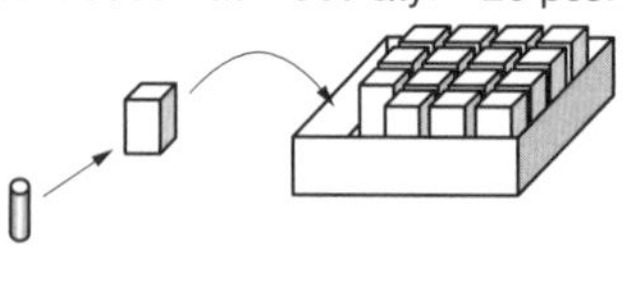

ワンポイントレッスン One-Point Advice

表示を見るのではなく、人の動き、設備、仕掛品、部品そのものを見ることで異常が分かるようにしたほうが効果的です。それに、図やグラフをたくさんつくらなくても済みます！

It is more effective for you to identify abnormalities through seeing operators' movement, machines, work pieces, and materials themselves, rather than reading charts and descriptions. At the same time, you will be freed from making burdensome charts!

Example of a Visualized Parts Presentation

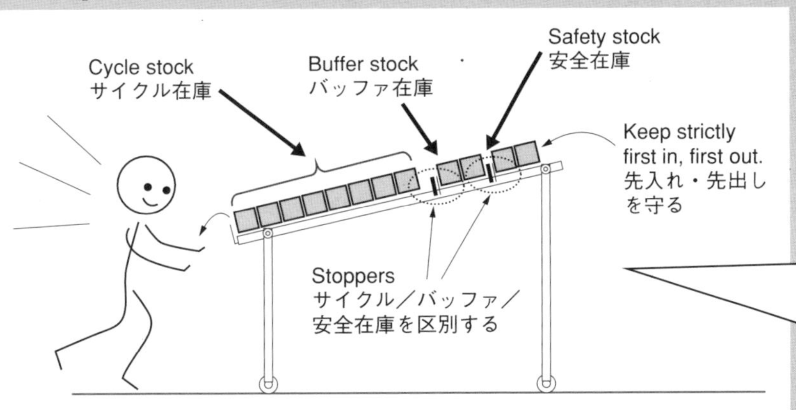

Instead of counting containers, we can see at a glance if it is the normal condition or not. In addition to the visibility, we can maintain FIFO quite easily with a flow rack.

Example of a Defects Presentation

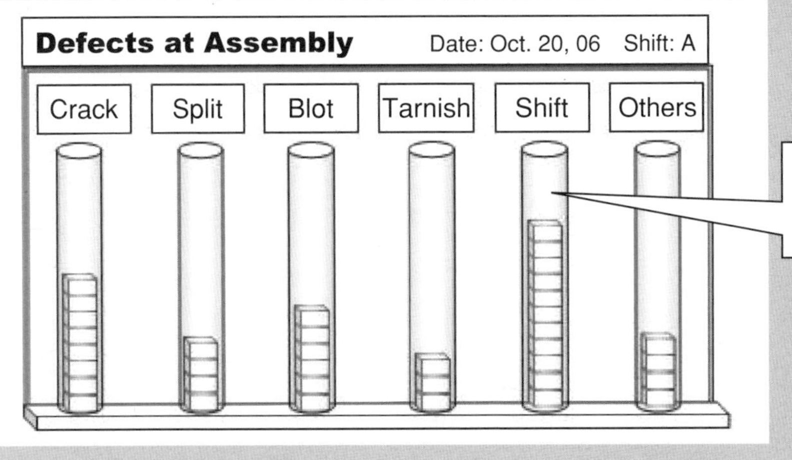

We can see at a glance which type of defect has been most frequently identified.

即座に対策を打ってこそ、目で見る管理の意味がある！
Making Things Visible Must Be Linked to Immediate Corrective Action!

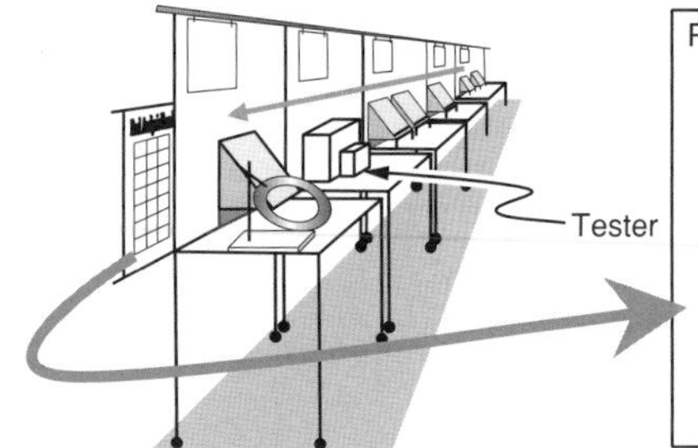

Production Analysis Board				Date: Jul. 21, 06	
Assembly Line # 01			Leader: Audrey Keane		
Required Qty.: 775 pcs./shift			Takt Time: 36 sec./p		
Time	Hourly		Cumulative		Problems/ Causes
	Planned	Actual	Planned	Actual	
08:00–09:00	100 /	100	100 /	100	
09:00–09:45	75 /	75	175 /	175	
10:00–11:00	100 /	60	275 /	235	Probe Broke
11:00–12:00	100 /	62	375 /	297	Unsolved
13:00–14:00	100 /	61	475 /	359	Unsolved

You should take countermeasures against problems immediately!

Let's talk 即座に対策を講じるべし！
Take countermeasures immediately!

A: 生産管理板をつくりました。時間単位の計画と実績が、誰にでもわかります。

A: We made this Production Analysis Board. Everybody can see the planned quantity versus the actual output on an hourly basis.

B: う〜ん。生産管理板自体は悪くないんだけど、何かおかしいところがあると思わない？

B: Um …The board itself is not wrong, but there is something incorrect. Don't you think so?

A: おかしいところ……？

A: Something incorrect …?

B: 時間当たり100個必要なんだよね？　10時から11時には、60個しかできなかった。

B: You need 100 pieces per hour, don't you? Between 10 and 11 o'clock, you had produced only 60 pieces.

A: はい。それは管理板からわかります。検査機の2つのプローブのうち、1つが壊れたのです。

A: Yes, we can see it from the board. One of two probes of the tester broke.

B: 続く11時から12時も62個。今、午後2時だよね。3時間以上、問題を放っておいたわけだ。

B: Then, between 11 and 12 o'clock, 62 pieces. It is 2:00 p.m. now. You have left problems unsolved for more than three hours!

A: ラインリーダーには修理はできません。

A: But, Line Leaders cannot repair the tester.

B: しょっちゅう壊れるなら、当面は交換用のプローブを準備しておいて、壊れたらすぐにラインリーダーが交換しなければいけない。それから、真因の解決も忘れずにね。

B: If it breaks so frequently, you must have some replacement-probes for a time and Line Leaders are required to change the broken probe immediately whenever it breaks. In addition, don't forget to resolve the root cause!

Chapter

5

改善に終わりなし
The Lean Journey

限量経営 —人と設備—

Genryo Management
—Labor Linearity and Capital Linearity

「限られた量」の人・モノ・金で安くつくって儲けること

限量(ゲンリョウ)は限られた資源という意味であり、限量経営とは、どのような経済環境においても確実に利益を出すようにするという考え方で、故・大野耐一氏の大切な教えのひとつです。経営者は、売上が伸びる時も伸びない時も、限られた経営資源でより安くモノをつくることで常に利益を出せる体質を維持するという責任を負わなければなりません。トヨタの強靭な利益体質は今や伝説的になっていますが、その利益体質を築く過程で、1950年代に倒産寸前まで追い込まれたトヨタの経営危機がいかに大きな影響を与えたかを思い起こすことが大事です。繊維産業で一時代を築いた豊田グループでしたが、第二次世界大戦後の壊滅的な経済状況にあった日本のすべての企業と同様に、20世紀初頭から繊維業界で蓄積してきた富を失った豊田もまた、厳しい国内市場で生き残るべく懸命に苦境と闘っていました。そのような環境下、豊田グループの指導者たちは、強くまた奥深い危機意識を持ち、いまだ発展途上にあってその潜在成長力さえ未知数だった国内自動車市場で日本の自動車メーカーとして確実に生き残るための非常に挑戦的な目標を設定しました。

Constraints in Resources to Meet Business Needs Is the Mother of the Toyota Way

"Genryo" means "limited resources" and "genryo management" was one of Taiichi Ohno's key management concepts to ensure profitability in any economic environment. Management should accept the responsibility to maintain profitability during periods of both growth and decline in sales by producing products at lower costs with limited use of resources. Though Toyota's great profitability has become legendary, it is important to remember how central the company's 1950 brush with bankruptcy was to its development. As was the case with all Japanese companies in the devastated post-WWII economy, the Toyoda group struggled greatly, having lost the wealth it had accumulated from the textile industry in the early 20th Century, while operating in a stringent Japanese economic environment. In these conditions, the leaders of the Toyoda group of companies experienced a profound sense of crisis and set aggressive targets to ensure their very survival as a Japanese automobile manufacturer with no capital funds while competing in the underdeveloped Japanese car market, a market whose potential was still unknown.

倹約すること、限られた資源を賢く使うことについて、日本人は世界的に有名ですが、かつてのような危機を知る者とてない21世紀の日本人にとって、「限量」は理解するのが難しい概念でしょう。そのようなわけで、TPSの他のコンセプトに比べて、「限量経営」は、議論されることも少ないし、人気もありません。しかしそれは、間違いなく、トヨタの底流にある製造業者としての強靭さの基礎をなすものの一つなのです。

While Japanese have a worldwide reputation for frugality and wise use of limited resources, genryo is a difficult concept to grasp for 21st Century Japanese who never experienced those troubled times. Genryo management, then, is less discussed or "popular" than other concepts of TPS, but is a foundation of Toyota's deep strength as a manufacturer.

このセクションでは、「限量経営」において、わけても特徴的な人の限量=「少人化」と、モノと金(設備投資)の限量=「段階的設備投資」を紹介します。(注:もう一つの限量であるモノと金(設備投資)の限量=「後工程引き取り」については、Chapter 2を参照して下さい)

In this section of *Kaizen Express*, we will discuss two key dimensions of genryo management: labor linearity and capital linearity. (Note: Use of material as a limited resource—"material linearity"—was covered in Chapter 2.)

焦土からの出発(1945～1956) Devastated war-torn Japan, 1945–1956

第2次世界大戦の敗北により、壊滅的な打撃を受けた戦後の日本経済には、わずかな資本しかなかった。当時、日本の産業が生き残る唯一の道は、アメリカ流の大量生産とは違うやり方を見つけ出すことだけだったのだ。当然ながら、豊田グループもまた事業資金不足に直面していた。

The devastated war-torn Japanese economy in the post-WWII period had little capital. The only ticket for survival in those days for Japanese industries was to find some alternative ways to the American way of mass production. Of course, the Toyoda Group also faced this shortage of funds.

限量経営とは、「売れ」に合わせて安くつくり、売上増でも売上減でも、必ず利益を出すこと
Genryo Management, or the Linearity of Labor, Material, and Capital

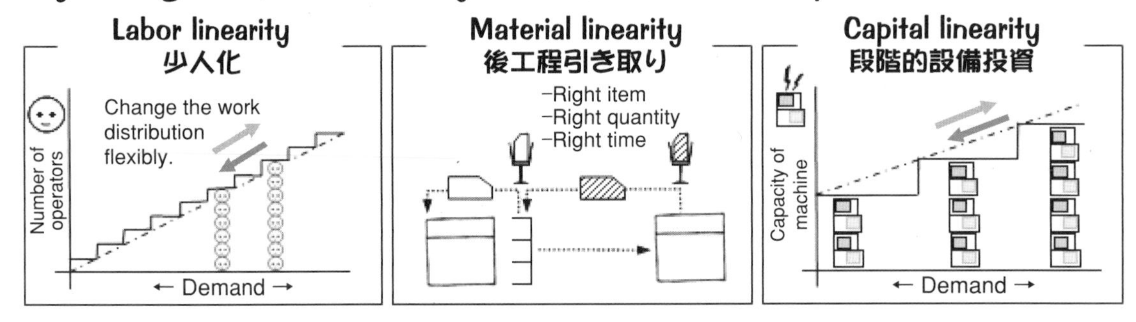

限量経営とは？

大野耐一氏の教えの1つ。限られた経営資源で安くモノをつくり、売上増でも売上減でも利益を出すという考え方と方法の体系（日本語で、“ゲン”は「限られた」、“リョウ”は「分量」という意味）。

What is genryo management?

Genryo management is a precept preached by Taiichi Ohno. It is a framework to make profits during periods of both growth and decline in sales through making products at lower costs with limited resources. (“Gen” means “limited” and “ryou” means “amount” in Japanese.)

少人化

需要の増減に合わせて作業者数を増やしたり減らしたりできるよう、作業者の配置を柔軟にするという考え方。これにより、需要の変化に対する単位生産当たりの作業者の人数を、かなりの程度、線形化することができる。遺憾ながら、需要減のときにラインの人数を減らすということが、私たちにはなかなかできないのだった。

Shojinka, or labor linearity

A philosophy for flexibly manning a production process so that the number of operators increases or decreases as the demand changes. This gives the process the approximate linearity of the amount of labor per unit (or part) produced as the demand changes. Regrettably, we often fail to adequately reduce the number of operators from the line when demand declines.

段階的設備投資

需要の変化に対して設備能力を少しずつ増やしたり除却したりできるよう、設備を小さな能力の単位で構想し、調達するという考え方。これにより、単位生産当たりの設備投資額を、ほとんど線形にすることができる。遺憾ながら私たちは、初期段階で能力が過大な設備を構想してしまうという失敗を繰り返してきた。

Capital linearity, or incremental investment

A philosophy for designing and purchasing machinery so that small amounts of capacity can be added or subtracted as demand changes. This gives the plant the approximate linearity of the amount of capital needed per unit (or part). Regrettably, we continue to design machines to have too much capacity in the initial stages.

ワンポイントレッスン One-Point Advice

なぜ段階的設備投資が有利なのか？
Advantage of Capital Linearity over Large-scale Investment

Assumption（前提条件）

You need to build up a capacity of 100,000 units of annual output. You have two options:
100,000台/年の能力増強が必要。道は２つ：

Option A

Large-scale model
大量生産モデル

大型・高速・多機能になりがちで、
その結果、高額
It tends to be large, high-volume, multi-functional, and accordingly expensive.

Option B

Linear model
段階的設備投資モデル

10,000
units/year

Cell-type layout

タクトタイムに合わせたシンプルで
小さな設備
It should simply meet estimated takt time requirements and should be small.

実際の需要量 Actual Demand	Option A	Option B
10万個超 Beyond 100,000 units	設備をもう１セット買うと、製品１個当たり投資額がハネ上がる If you get another new set of machines, the capital investment per unit would be significantly high.	需要増１万個ごとに、必要に応じて設備を追加することができる You can add the lines as required with each 10,000 units of capacity.
10万個以下 Less than 100,000 units	能力を小さくすることはほぼ不可能、現下の効率を維持することもできない It will be almost impossible to decrease capacity and keep efficiency at the current level.	需要に合わせて設備を止め、能力を小さくすることができる You can subtract capacity by shutting down as many lines as required.

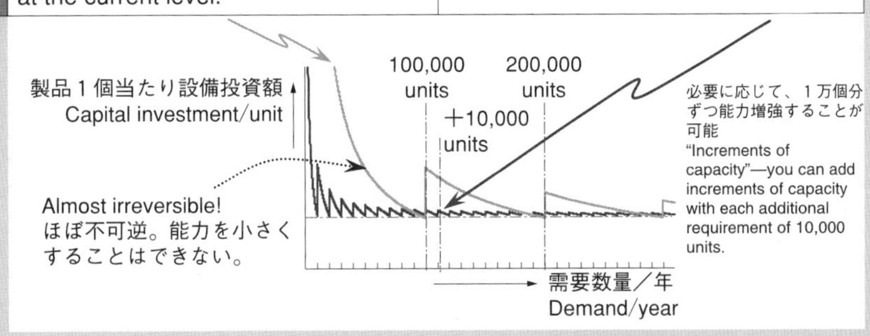

構想段階から設備を変えよう！ How Do You Design and Lay Out Your Machines?

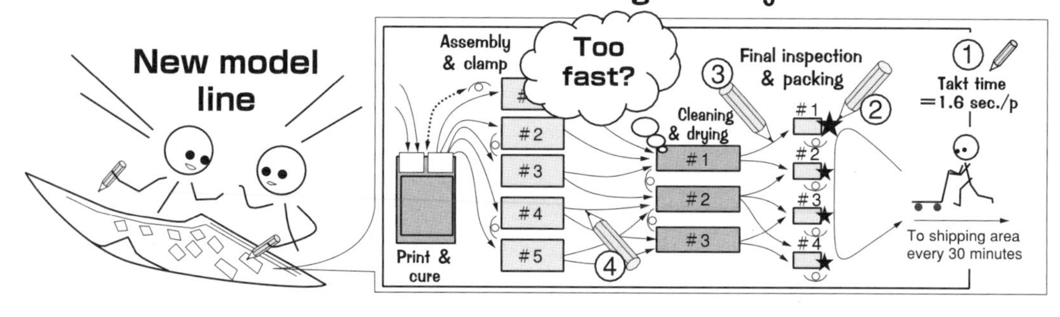

Let's talk いつでもどこでも「整流」を目指すべし！ Regulate your production flow, everywhere, all the time!

A: これが今度の新製品の製造ラインの構想図です。リーンの考え方をちょっと採り入れたつもりです。必要数は月に100万個、3シフトで20日稼働として、タクトタイムは1.6秒に1個です。

A: This is our draft of new-model production lines. We intend to bring in some lean concepts. We need to produce one million pieces every month, so assuming 20 operating days every month with three shifts, takt time is 1.6 second per piece.

B: なるほど、工程がちょっとは連結されてるね。えーっと…このレイアウト図上で、最終製品が完成する場所に印を付けてみて？

B: I can see that some of the processes are connected. Well, on this chart, mark up all of the final processes where finished goods are completed.

A: ここと、ここと… 4カ所。最終工程は、検査機と梱包です。

A: One, two, ——there are four points. The final process is inspection and packing.

B: その前は？ どこから来るの？ 何カ所あるかな？ 検査・梱包から前工程まで、それぞれ線でつないでみて。

B: Where does each work piece come from? How many sources are there? Line up from each inspection-packing process to its source.

A: えーとですね、レイアウト図では、前工程の洗浄・乾燥機が…3台。…あれ？ なぜ3台にしちゃったんだろう？ 4台で検査・梱包と直結した方がよかったのに…。

A: Let's see. On our drawing, we have three cleaning-drying machines upstream. Hmm, why did we set three? We should set four cleaning-drying machines and connect them directly to each tester.

B: ああ、洗浄・乾燥機1台当たりの能力が大き過ぎるからだよ。単純に必要数を能力で割れば3台だよね。どうすればよいと思う？

B: Ah, I see. Because its capacity is too much, you got the result "three," simply dividing the demand by its capacity. What can you do here?

全員参加 ―実践会、創意くふう提案制度―

Employee Involvement
―Practical Kaizen Training & Suggestion Programs

人の力を引き出そう！

全員を改善活動に巻き込む

お客様が求めるものを、求めるときに、求める量だけ提供することができる流れをつくりたいと願うなら、会社の内外を貫く流れに関係するすべての人々に、自ら進んで働き方を変えてもらわなければなりません。時期の違いや関与の深い浅いはあっても、全員を巻き込むことが不可欠です。

指示に従うだけではもったいない

人間はとてもフレキシブルで、大きな能力を持っています。ひとたびトヨタ生産方式の考え方を知り、基本的な手法を身に付けたなら、自ら改善に貢献したいと考えるようになるはずです。

力を結集するには

トヨタ生産方式に学び、改革を進めようという活動は、トップダウンで始まるものかもしれません。しかし、改革は1人でできるものではなく、また、上から指示しただけでうまく動くものでもありません。そこで、人々の能力を引き出し、力を結集することが大切になるのです。いわゆる方針展開とともに、人々の能力を引き出すための実践的な教育訓練や改善サークル、改善提案制度が欠かせないのです。

Why Employee Involvement?

What is employee involvement?

If you are eager to realize a production flow that can provide the right item at the right time in the right quantity as required by your customers, you should motivate everyone connected to the flow to want to change for themselves the way they do their work. Their involvement is crucial to your success, even though there may be differences in the amount of time it takes and the level of their engagement.

People's latent potential

People are very flexible and have great abilities. Once they understand the way of thinking and trained themselves in the basic arts of TPS, most of them will be willing to contribute something to kaizen.

How to concentrate people's efforts

A lean conversion may be started as a top-down process in many companies. However, nobody can realize it by him/herself and any new system cannot run well only by orders from above. Therefore, both enhancing people's abilities and directing them appropriately are absolutely necessary. Practical kaizen training programs, kaizen circle activities, and suggestion programs are needed together with policy deployment.

方針展開に沿った実践的なプログラムで、働く人の能力を引き出そう！

Enhance People's Ability through Practical Programs to Support Policy Deployment

- **Kaizen workshops** 実践会
- **Kaizen circle activities** 改善サークル活動
- **Suggestion programs** 提案制度

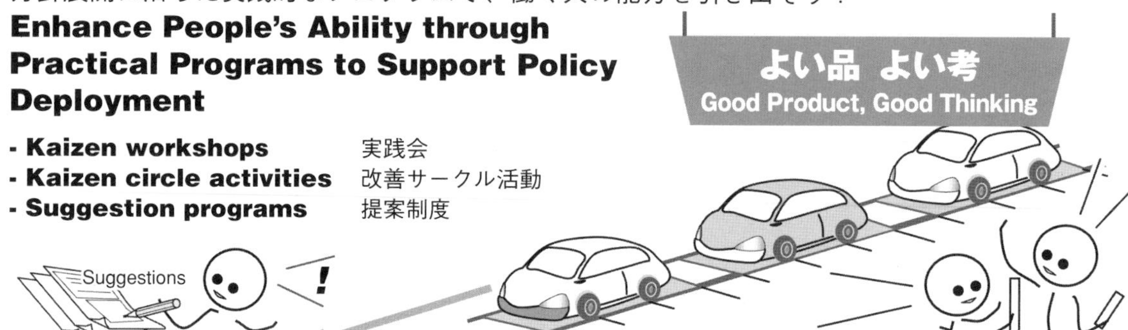

実践会で学ぶ

教室での座学は、もちろんある程度は必要ですが、改善は実践を通して学ぶものです。
実践会では、自分の職場の改善テーマと改善の方法を自分たちで決めるところから始めて、限られた時間内で実践し、成果をまとめて発表することで、改善を学ぶことができます。また、次の改善テーマを見つけ出すよい機会ともなるでしょう。

Learning to do kaizen through kaizen workshops

Of course we need some study in classrooms, but kaizen is to be learned through actual practice.
You can really learn to do kaizen in practical kaizen workshops, starting with setting your own targets and selecting methods, practicing them at your workplace in a set period of time, and making a presentation. It will also be a good opportunity to find out your next challenges.

改善サークル活動

小集団活動は、日本的な手法として最も有名なものかもしれませんが、単に小集団をつくっただけでは、うまく動きません。グループは方針展開に沿った明確な目標を持ち、管理者は彼らを正しくサポートしなければなりません。数字よりも、活動を通してメンバーの能力を高めることが大切です。

Kaizen circle activities

Small group activity may be the most famous method of the Japanese way of management, but it will not work automatically just by setting up groups. Groups should have clear goals under your policy deployment and managers should carefully support them. It is more important to enhance team-members' ability than to chase metrics.

創意くふう提案制度

トヨタの工場を見学すると、「よい品 よい考」と書かれた大きな横断幕が頭上に掲げられているのに気づくでしょう。トヨタは、「創意くふう提案制度」を1951年に始め、今も多くの提案が従業員から寄せられています。改善提案制度は、人々を改善活動に巻き込むのに、大きな力となるはずです。

Suggestion programs

You can see large banners saying "Good Product, Good Thinking" overhead in any Toyota plant. Toyota started their suggestion program named "Sou-i Kufuh Tei-an Se-i-do" in 1951 and Toyota employees still contribute suggestions through this program. A suggestion program can be a great way to involve workers in your lean conversion.

ワンポイントトレッスン One-Point Advice

活動管理板をつくろう！倦(う)まず弛(たゆ)まず改善を続けるべし

A Well-Used Project Tracking Board Can Bring a Continuous Kaizen Culture to Your Workplace!

いわゆる活動管理板。「見せる化」になってしまうと困りものですが、そこで働く人々に現状を理解してもらい、協力してもらうのに、大きな力となるでしょう。この種の活動管理板がなければ、つくりましょう。

Just to “make things visual” is not your true objective, but a Project Tracking Board will stand by you to encourage every employee to understand the situation and contribute to the improvement activity. If you do not have this type of board yet, you should make one right away!

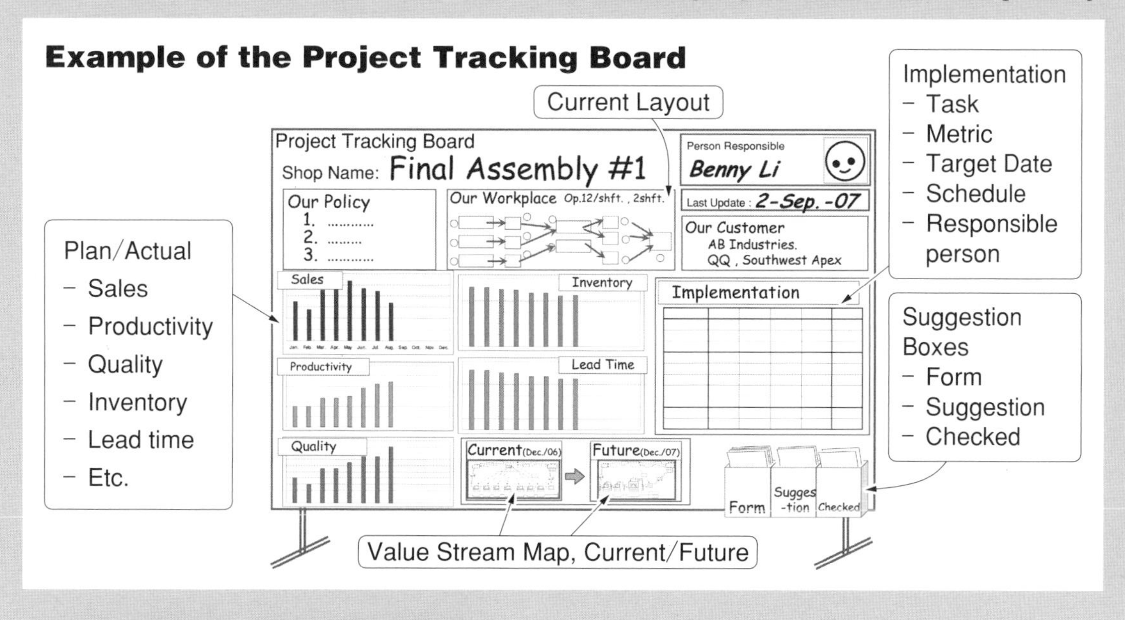

覚えておこう！ Remember!

実践会は、どう進める？

How to Promote the Kaizen Workshop

５日間の実践トレーニングがよく知られていますが、週に１回あるいは２週間に１回の社内実践会も効果的です。対象の職場、目標、実践、発表と評価、次の課題の発見について、管理者はきちんとサポートしなければなりません。

The five-day kaizen workshop may be more famous, but it is also effective to hold a one-day kaizen workshop every week or fortnightly. Managers should fully support the process by selecting the target workplaces, setting goals, implementing, presenting and evaluating, and identifying next challenges.

12th Kaizen Workshop
05-Sep.-07

- Time Table
  - 10:00 - Opening session
  - 10:30 - Practice
  - 16:00 - Closing session
- Workplaces
  - Final Assembly #1 - #4
  - Shipping Dept.

進め方は、ボトム-トップ-ボトムで！
The Process Should Become "Bottom-Top-Bottom"

キャッチボール
を繰り返すべし

What do we know? What is the problem?
Why are we talking about it?
What are we doing about it?

改善は私が！

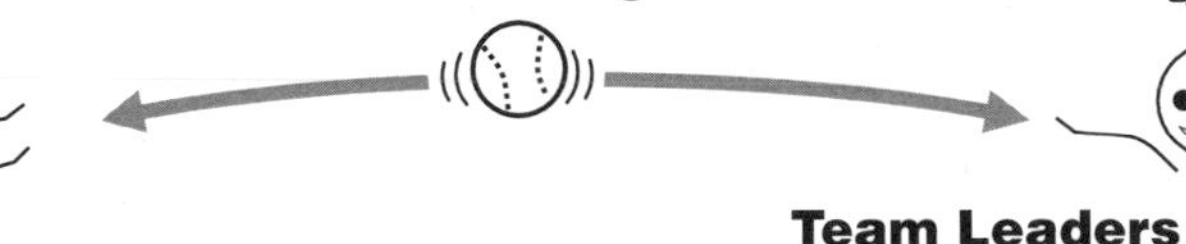

Manager

Team Leaders

Let's talk 自ら考え、実行するチームをつくろう！
Build kaizen teams that think for themselves and take initiative to do kaizen on their own!

A: 毎月実践会を開催していますが、表面的で、ときどき後戻りしてしまうんです。

A: We hold a kaizen workshop once a month, but I am afraid they might not be substantive enough because sometimes things revert back to the old way after awhile.

B: もっと詳しく話してくれますか？ 前回は何をしたの？ どんな改善をやったのか、具体的に教えてください。

B: Can you be more specific? What did you do last time? Exactly what kaizen did you do?

A: 設備を移動して直線ラインを変形U字ラインにしたんです。でも、改善チームは何をすべきかをなかなか決められなくて、結局、私が言ってしまったんです。それで、今は改善が後戻りしています。

A: We moved equipment from a straight line to a modified U-shape. But, the team had much trouble deciding what to do, so finally I had to tell them. And now the improvements are already regressing.

B: なるほど。君が「これをやりなさい」と言ってしまったんだね。どうして彼らが自分でよいアイデアにたどり着くようにもっていけなかったのかな？

B: I see. So, you told them what to do. Why couldn't you get them to come up with their own good ideas?

A: 彼らはまだ原理原則がわかっていないようなんです。私が答えを言わなければ、彼らは間違ったことをしてしまったでしょう。あるいは、試行錯誤を通して正しい解を得ようとすれば、もっと時間がかかっていたと思います。

A: They still don't seem to get some basic concepts. If I didn't tell them the answer, they would've made a mistake. Or it would take a long time for them to find the right answer through trial and error.

B: しかしね、それをやらなくちゃいけないんだ。君は、1個流しをやってリードタイムを短縮してもらいたかったんだよね？ 後戻りしてしまうのはなぜなのか、なぜ彼らが1個流しをやれないのか、君がもっとよく考えなくてはいけないよ。

B: Still, you have to try. You wanted them to use one-piece flow to shorten the lead time, right? Think more about why they revert to the old way. Why can't they implement one-piece flow??

わたしたちの改善

Develop Your Own Kaizen Guidelines!

倦(う)まず弛(たゆ)まず改善を続ける組織になろう！

さらなる改善を！

１つ改善ができたら、その現場をもう一度よく見ましょう。人の手待ち、工程間の仕掛り、工程がつながっていないといった問題がまだあることに気づくはずです。次は、何をしたらよいでしょう？あなたにはもうそれがわかっているし、きっと実現できるはずです。

改善し続ける仕組みを築く

常にムダを探し、すぐに「廃除する」という意識と行動規範を、職場の人々が持たなければ、どのような改善も後退してしまいます。難しいと感じるかもしれませんが、ひとたび改善の意義を実感したなら、人々は、よりよい仕事のやり方を自ら追求するようになるでしょう。管理者は、彼らをていねいにサポートしなければなりません。

継続的改善が人を育てる

自ら現場を見て問題を発見し、自ら考えて改善を実践する、というサイクルを繰り返すことが、改善を理解し、力をつけるためのかけがえのない訓練の場となるのです。

Let's Build a Continuous Improvement Process Within Your Team!

Self-reflection and further improvement

After implementing kaizen at your workplace, you should carefully observe it again. You can probably still see people waiting, work pieces stagnating between processes, some processes isolated, and the rest. What do you do next? You already know what the problem is and what needs to be done. This is your chance to try some new ideas.

Building kaizen into your team

If people at your workplace don't have the mind-sets and behaviors to always try to identify and eliminate wastes immediately, any kaizen will regress. You might find it difficult, but once people have really understood the significance of kaizen, then they will be willing to pursue a better way of working by themselves. Managers need to support them with patience.

Developing people's ability through continuous improvement

The process of the continuous improvement (CI) cycle of seeing the workplace, identifying problems, and implementing solutions figured out by yourselves, can be an invaluable opportunity to understand kaizen and develop your ability.

継続的改善を、仕事の中に埋め込むべし！
Building Your Own Continuous Improvement Process Is Essential to Realize a Successful Lean Transformation!

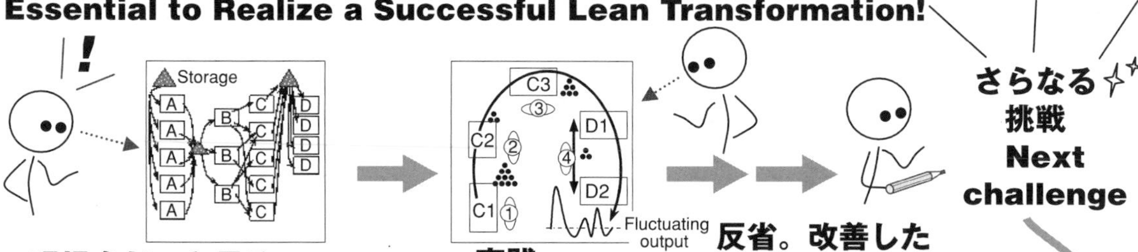

自分の改善ガイドラインを持とう！ …… Develop your own kaizen guidelines!

誰かに言われてやる改善ではなく、自分たちのものとして改善を考えることが大切です。このために、まず、自分たちの改善ガイドラインをつくってみるとよいでしょう。

Instead of kaizen directed by someone else, you must personally understand it as your own process. An important step to gain a sense of kaizen ownership: you should develop your own kaizen guidelines by yourself!

どんなガイドライン？ …… What kind of guideline do you develop?

トヨタ生産方式の本は、書店にいくらでもありますね。同じようなものをつくろうとするのは時間のムダというものかもしれません。しかし、あなたの現場で、あなたが実際にやった改善をもとに、毎日の仕事に役立つ指針をつくるのなら、それはたいへん意義深いことです。ここでは、美しく整った教科書を追求してもあまり意味はないでしょう。

There are plenty of TPS books in the bookstores. It might be just a waste of time these days to create yet another similar one. But, it could be very helpful for you to create guidelines based on your own achievements at the workplace to really help your everyday work. Then it may not be so useful to seek some sort of sophisticated textbook.

どこから始める？ …… Where do we start?

あなたはすでに、ライン改善の経験も、後工程引き取りの経験もあるはずです。あなたがたどった道を振り返って書き出してみましょう。

Begin with your own experiences, such as improving production lines or establishing supermarkets with pull systems. Start by retracing and describing the route you took.

誰のために？ …… Who will use your guidelines?

ガイドラインをつくるとき、それはあなたの職場の仲間のため、あなたの後に続く人のためであること、そしてなにより、あなた自身が自分の改善を振り返り、より深く問題を理解するためのものであることをいつも忘れないで下さい。

In developing the guidelines, please remember that it is to be for your colleagues, for your successors, and especially for yourself to reflect on your kaizen experience and to understand even more deeply the problems you have overcome.

ワンポイントレッスン One-Point Advice

組立ラインの改善ガイドラインをつくってみよう！

Making Your Kaizen Guideline to Improve Assembly Lines

- **Make it simple and easy to understand with illustrations.**（わかりやすく）
- **Standardize as much as possible.**（常に標準化を目指すべし）

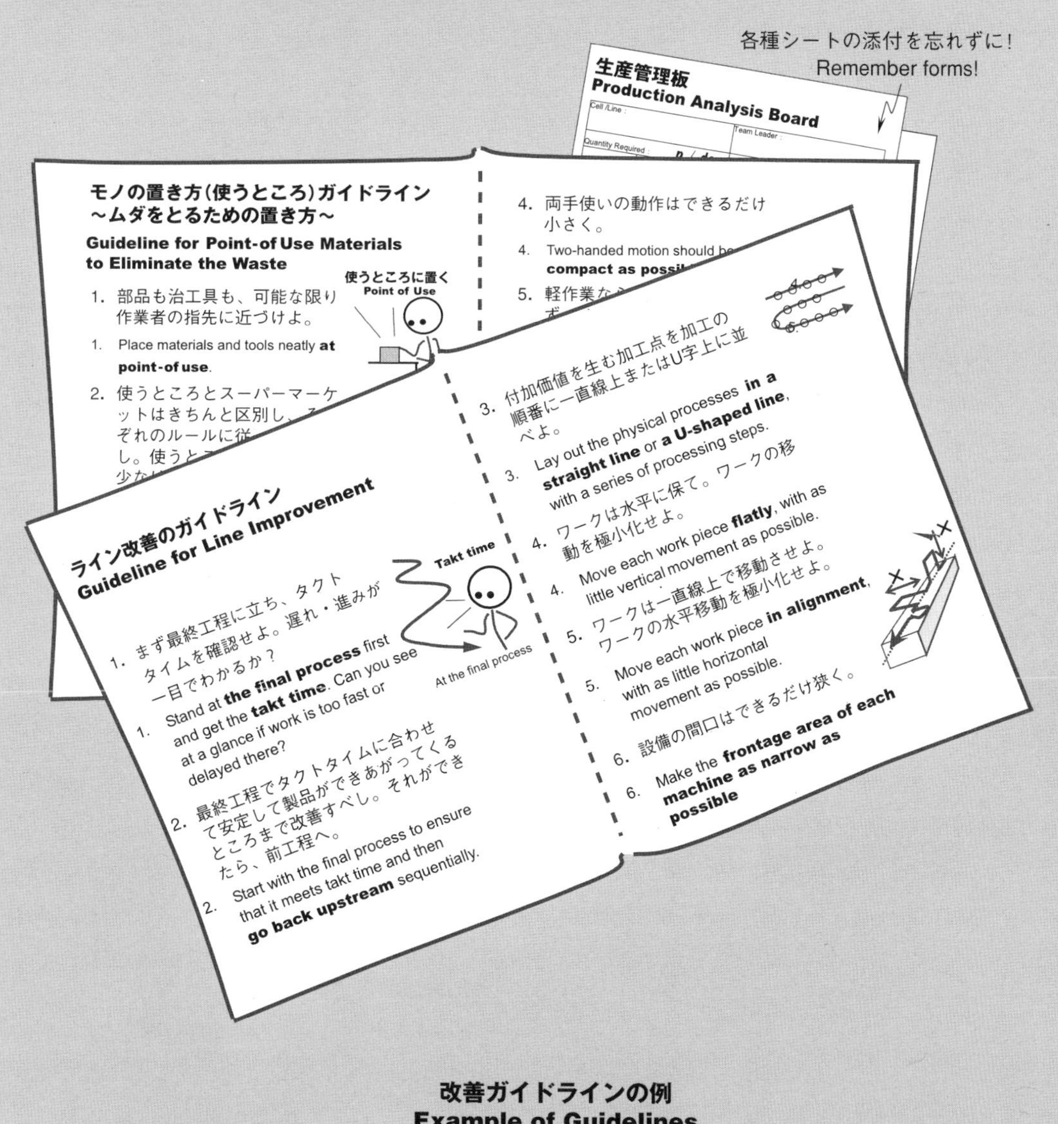

改善ガイドラインの例
Example of Guidelines

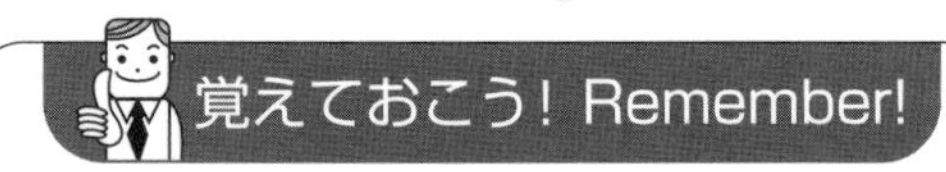

「何か質問はありますか？」から一歩も二歩も踏み出そう！

職場では、改善に関することのみならず、いろいろなことが毎日「説明」されているはずです。大切なことを説明した後で、「何か質問はありますか？」と聞いていませんか？　そして、人々は「いいえ、質問はありません」と繰り返しているのでは？　これでは、本当に伝わったかどうか、わかったものではありません。では、どうしたらよいのでしょう？　たとえば「今の説明から、あなたがわかったことを教えて下さい」と質問してみたらどうでしょう？　常に双方向のコミュニケーションを心がけましょう！

Beyond Just Asking "Any Questions?"

We often must explain many things related not only to kaizen but to other important issues (like safety, engineering process changes, or QC procedures for new models). Do you ask "do you have any questions?" after explaining something important and people respond just saying "No, we don't"? This is far from the most effective instruction. What questions might be more effective here? How about asking "please let me know what you've learned about this issue from my explanation"? Always look for interactive communication!

人を尊重することが改善の基盤
Respecting People Is Always the Basis of Your Kaizen

How do we change from "command" to "commitment"?
命令から約束へ

From boss-and-subordinates to "team members"
肩書きではなく、
ともに働く仲間として語り合おう

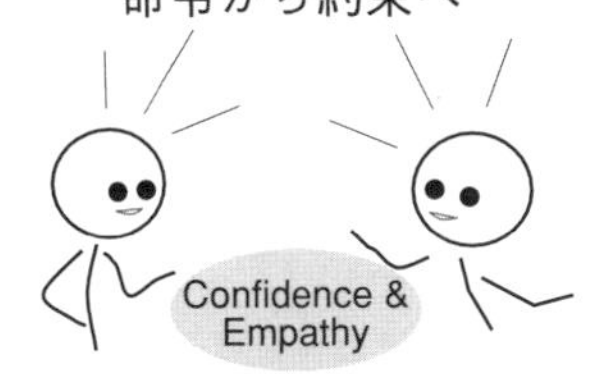

Esteem his/her valuable time
ともに働く人の時間を大切に

Let's talk 一番よくわかっている人に教えてもらおう！ Ask the person closest to the problem!

A: 外観不良のキズが減らなくて困っています。

B: なるほど、パレート図もあるし、傾向も把握してるね。確か、外観検査担当はメアリーだよね？　彼女こそ、問題に最も近いところにいる人。彼女と話してみるのが一番だよ。彼女が何を知っているか、君は聞いてる？

A: えーとですね…、不良があったら報告を受けていますが、メアリーの考えをきちんと聞いたことはありませんでした。そうですよね、メアリーに聞いてみましょう！

A: メアリー、おはよう！

M: おはよう！　今日はどんな話？

A: メアリー、キズ不良について、気がついていることを教えてくれないかな？

M: キズね。今も１つあったわ。リーダーには言ったんだけど、カシメ機でキズが起きるような気がしてる。でも、どのヘッドが悪いかはわからないの。まとめて箱に入って出てくるでしょ。で、順番がバラバラになっちゃうから…。

A: ありがとう、メアリー！　知らなかったよ。今まできちんと君の話を聞かなくてごめんなさい。

M: え？　知らなかったの？　不良のことなら、もっと言わなきゃいけないことがあるわよ！

A: We are currently in trouble with cosmetic defects: scratches.

B: Let me see … Oh, I can see the trend from this Pareto chart. Hmm. The Appearance Inspector is Mary, right? She is the one closest to this problem and would be the best person to talk to. Have you asked her what she knows?

A: Um … I receive a report when each defect occurs, but I just realized that I had never asked her exactly. Let's ask for her help.

A: Hi, Mary! Good morning! How are you today?

M: Good morning! What's up today?

A: Mary, please tell us what you think about the scratch defects.

M: Scratches? I found one just now. As I've told the Team Leader, I think it might occur at the crimper. But, we can't identify which crimp-head made it. Parts are ejected into a batch box, so the sequence is not kept there.

A: Thanks, Mary! I didn't know that. I'm sorry I didn't ask you sooner.

M: Really? Didn't you know that?! I have much more I can tell you about our defects!

改善フォーム集
Forms

Production Analysis Board 生産管理板

Line/Cell Name:	Team Leader:	Date:
Quantity Required:	Takt Time:	Shift:
		Num of Operator:

Time	Hourly	Cumulative	Problem/Causes	Sign-off
	Plan / Actual	Plan / Actual		
: ～ :	/	/		
: ～ :	/	/		
: ～ :	/	/		
: ～ :	/	/		
: ～ :	/	/		
: ～ :	/	/		
: ～ :	/	/		
: ～ :	/	/		
: ～ :	/	/		
: ～ :	/	/		
: ～ :	/	/		
: ～ :	/	/		
: ～ :	/	/		
: ～ :	/	/		
: ～ :	/	/		

Example of Production Analysis Board (生産管理板の例)

A Production Analysis Board is a display that must be located at the exit of the cell (or the line) to show actual performance compared with planned performance on an hourly basis.

生産管理板とは、時間単位に出来高の計画と実績を表示する掲示板です。セルまたはラインの出口に必ず設置しましょう。

Production Analysis Board

Line/Cell Name: Final Assembly #7		Team Leader: Benny Li		Date: April 07
Quantity Required: 690 p		Takt Time: 40 sec./p		Shift: A Num of Operator: 16
Time	Hourly Plan/Actual	Cumulative Plan/Actual	Problem/Causes	Sign-off
06:00〜07:00	90 / 90	90 / 90		Sharon
07:00〜08:00	90 / 88	180 / 178	Tester Minor Stoppage	Sharon
08:00〜09:00	90 / 90	270 / 268		Sharon
09:10〜10:10	90 / 85	360 / 353	Defects (Appearance)	Sharon
10:10〜11:10	90 / 90	450 / 443		Roy
11:40〜12:40	90 / 90	540 / 533		Sharon
12:40〜13:40	90 / 86	630 / 619	Defects (Bad Parts)	Sharon
13:50〜14:30	60 / 60	690 / 679		Sharon
O.T.	11 / 11	690 / 690		Roy

Supervisor signs hourly

Remember breaks

Area Manager signs at lunch and end of shift

Just keeping visibility is not our real objective. Problems must be linked to corrective action!

Process Study Sheet（作業分析シート）

Process Study	Process:	Product:	Observer:	Date/Time:	Page /

Process Steps	OPERATOR												MACHINE Cycle Time	Notes
	Work Element	Observed Times										Repeatable		
		1	2	3	4	5	6	7	8	9	10			

Example of Process Study Sheet （作業分析の例）

Process Study	Process: Final Assembly #7	Product: DV-020332	Observer: Benny	Date/Time: April 18, 2007 14:00	Page 1/3

Process Steps	OPERATOR												MACHINE Cycle Time	Notes
	Work Element	Observed Times										Repeatable		
		1	2	3	4	5	6	7	8	9	10			
Assembly 1	Get base & put into fixture	4	5	6	3	4	4	4	4	5	4	4		Base far away
	Get pin & put into fixture	6	8	10	15	9	10	10	7	11	10	10		Fixture unstable
	Put fixture into machine	2	2	1	2	2	3	2				2		
	Machine cycle	1	1	1								1	6	Operator waiting
	Remove	2	2	2	1	2	2					2		
	Check appearance & place	8	11	8	20	7	8	9	9	9	8	8		Checking unstable
	Subtotal											27		
Assembly 2	Get lower case													
	Get work piece													
	Put into lower cas													Insertion unstable
	Get upper case &													
	Put into forming m													Machine gate far away
	...													
	...													

Timing Tips
- Collect real times at the process.
- Position yourself so you can see the operator's hand motions.
- Time each work element separately.
- Time several cycles of each work element.
- Observe an operator who is qualified to perform the job.
- Always separate operator time and machine time.
- Select the lowest repeatable time for each element.
- Remember shop floor courtesy.

Operator Balance Chart（OBC）（作業者バランスチャート）

Process:	Product:	Takt Time:	Date/Time:	Notes

①　②　③　④　⑤　⑥　⑦　⑧　⑨

Process										
Time										

Example of Operator Balance Chart (OBC) (作業者バランスチャートの例)

Process:	Product:	Takt Time:	Date/Time:	Notes: *Kaizen Workshop #10*
Final Assembly #7	*AB010*	*38*	*Mar. 20, 2007*	*Operator Saving: 1*

タクトタイムは
必ず**赤い線**で記入！
Takt Time should be lined in **red** ink

Current Situation

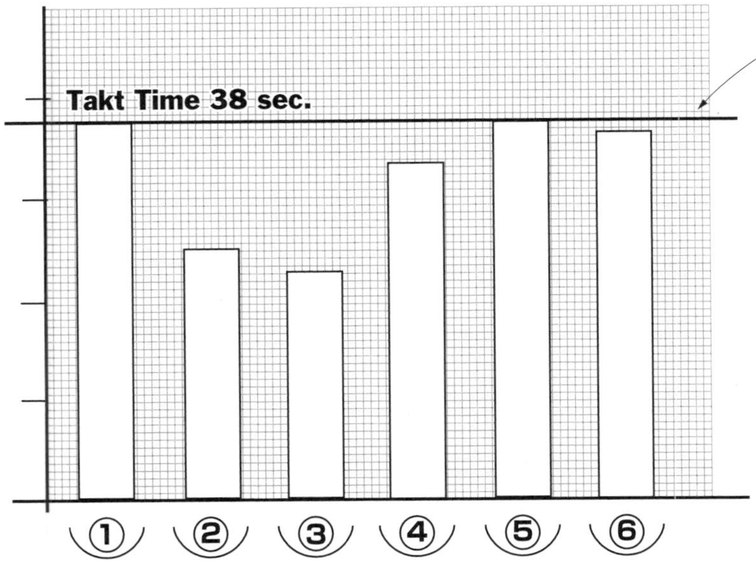

Process	*Assemble 1*	*Assemble 2*	*Forming*	*Assemble 3*	*Tester*	*Appr.*	*Total*
Time	*38*	*25*	*22*	*33*	*38*	*37*	*193*

After Kaizen

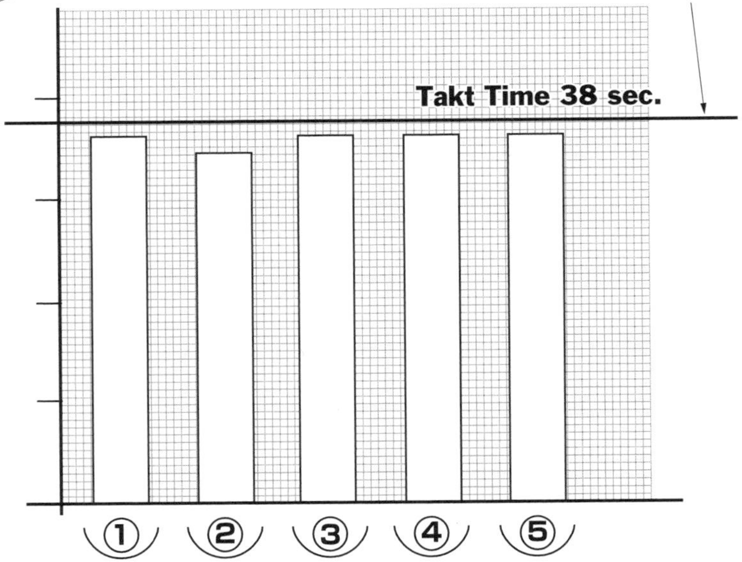

Assemble 1	*Forming*	*Assemble 2*	*Tester*	*Appr.*	*Total*
37	*36*	*37*	*37*	*37*	*184*

Standardized Work 1: Process Capacity Sheet

（標準作業1：工程別能力表）

Process Capacity Sheet	Approved by:	Part #	Application	Entered by:	Date
		Part name	Number of parts	Line	

Step	Step name	Machine #	BASIC TIME			TOOL CHANGE		PROCESSING CAPACITY/SHIFT	Remarks
			MANUAL	AUTO	COMPLETION	CHANGE	TIME		
		Total							

Example of Process Capacity Sheet (工程別能力表の例)

Process Capacity Sheet	Approved by: R. Quan	Part # 25-59001	Application JN-01	Entered by: Wayne Xi	Date May 08, 2007
		Part name Base Unit	Number of parts 1	Line Machine Shop #2	

Step	Step name	Machine #	BASIC TIME			TOOL CHANGE		PROCESSING CAPACITY/SHIFT	Remarks
			MANUAL	AUTO	COMPLETION	CHANGE	TIME		
1	Cut	C100	6	32	38	500	2 min.	720 p	
2	Rough Grind	GR100	7	12	19	1,000	5 min.	1,440 p	
3	Fine Grind	GR200	7	30	37	200	5 min.	724 p	
4	Measure Diameter	TS100	8	4	12	—	—	2,325 p	
		Total	28						

The Process Capacity Chart is used to calculate the capacity of each machine to confirm true capacity and to identify and eliminate bottlenecks. Processing capacity per shift will be calculated from the available production time, completion time, and tool-change time (and other factors as necessary) for each work piece.

工程別能力表は、生産能力を正しく把握してボトルネックを見つけ、改善するために、個々の設備の能力を計算するために使うものです。加工能力は、稼働時間、部品1個あたりの完成時間と刃具交換時間から計算します（必要に応じて、その他の条件を考慮する場合もあります）。

Standardized Work 2: Standardized Work Combination Table

(標準作業2: 標準作業組み合わせ票)

Standardized Work Combination Table	From:	Date:	Required Units per Shift:	—— Hand
	To:	Area:	Takt Time:	∿∿∿ Walk
				—— Auto

	Work Elements	Time (sec.)			Seconds																			
		Hand	Auto	Walk	5	10	15	20	25	30	35	40	45	50	55	60	65	70	75	80	85	90	95	100
1																								
2																								
3																								
4																								
5																								
6																								
7																								
8																								
9																								
10																								
11																								
12																								
13																								
14																								
15																								
	Totals		Waiting		5	10	15	20	25	30	35	40	45	50	55	60	65	70	75	80	85	90	95	100
					Seconds																			

Example of Standardized Work Combination Table

（標準作業組み合わせ票の例）

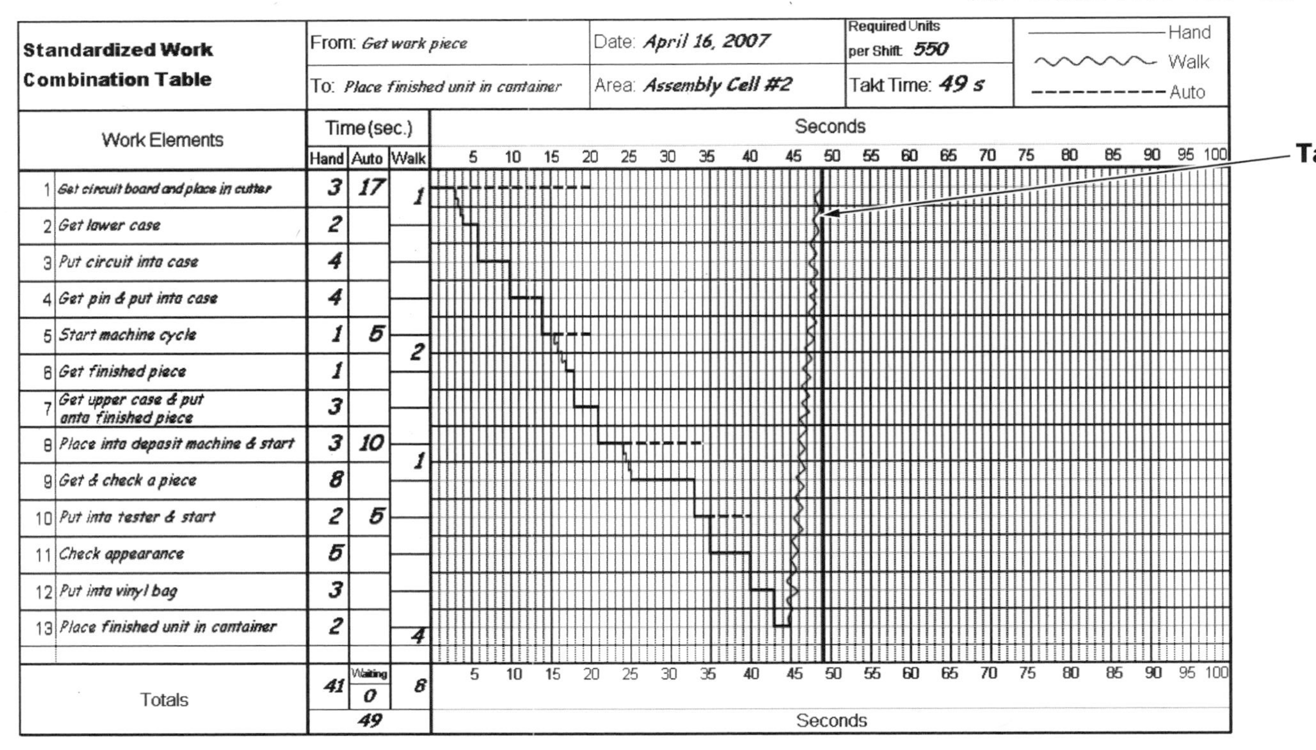

Standardized Work Combination Table	From: Get work piece	Date: April 16, 2007	Required Units per Shift: 550	—— Hand
	To: Place finished unit in container	Area: Assembly Cell #2	Takt Time: 49 s	~~~ Walk / - - - Auto

	Work Elements	Hand	Auto	Walk
1	Get circuit board and place in cutter	3	17	1
2	Get lower case	2		
3	Put circuit into case	4		
4	Get pin & put into case	4		
5	Start machine cycle	1	5	2
6	Get finished piece	1		
7	Get upper case & put onto finished piece	3		
8	Place into deposit machine & start	3	10	1
9	Get & check a piece	8		
10	Put into tester & start	2	5	
11	Check appearance	5		
12	Put into vinyl bag	3		
13	Place finished unit in container	2		4
	Totals	41	Waiting 0	8
		49		

The Standardized Work Combination Table shows the combination of manual work time, walk time, and machine processing time for each operation in a production sequence. This form is a more precise process design tool than the Operator Balance Chart. It can be very helpful to identify the waste of waiting and overburden, and to confirm standard work-in-process.

標準作業組み合わせ票を見れば、ラインの作業者ごとに、作業順序に沿って人と機械の組み合わせがどうなっているのかがよくわかります。これは、先に説明した「作業者バランスチャート」よりも精緻な工程設計ツールと言えるでしょう。手待ちのムダやムリを発見したり、標準手持ちを決めるのにも役立ちます。

Standardized Work 3: Standardized Work Chart （標準作業3: 標準作業票）

Standardized Work Chart	From: / To:	Date:	Prepared By:	Dept. /Location:	Team Leader:	Supervisor:

Quality Check ◇	Safety Precaution ✚	Standard Work-in-Process: Symbol ●	Standard Work-in-Process: Number of WIP	Takt Time	Cycle Time	Operator Number

Example of Standardized Work Chart (標準作業票の例)

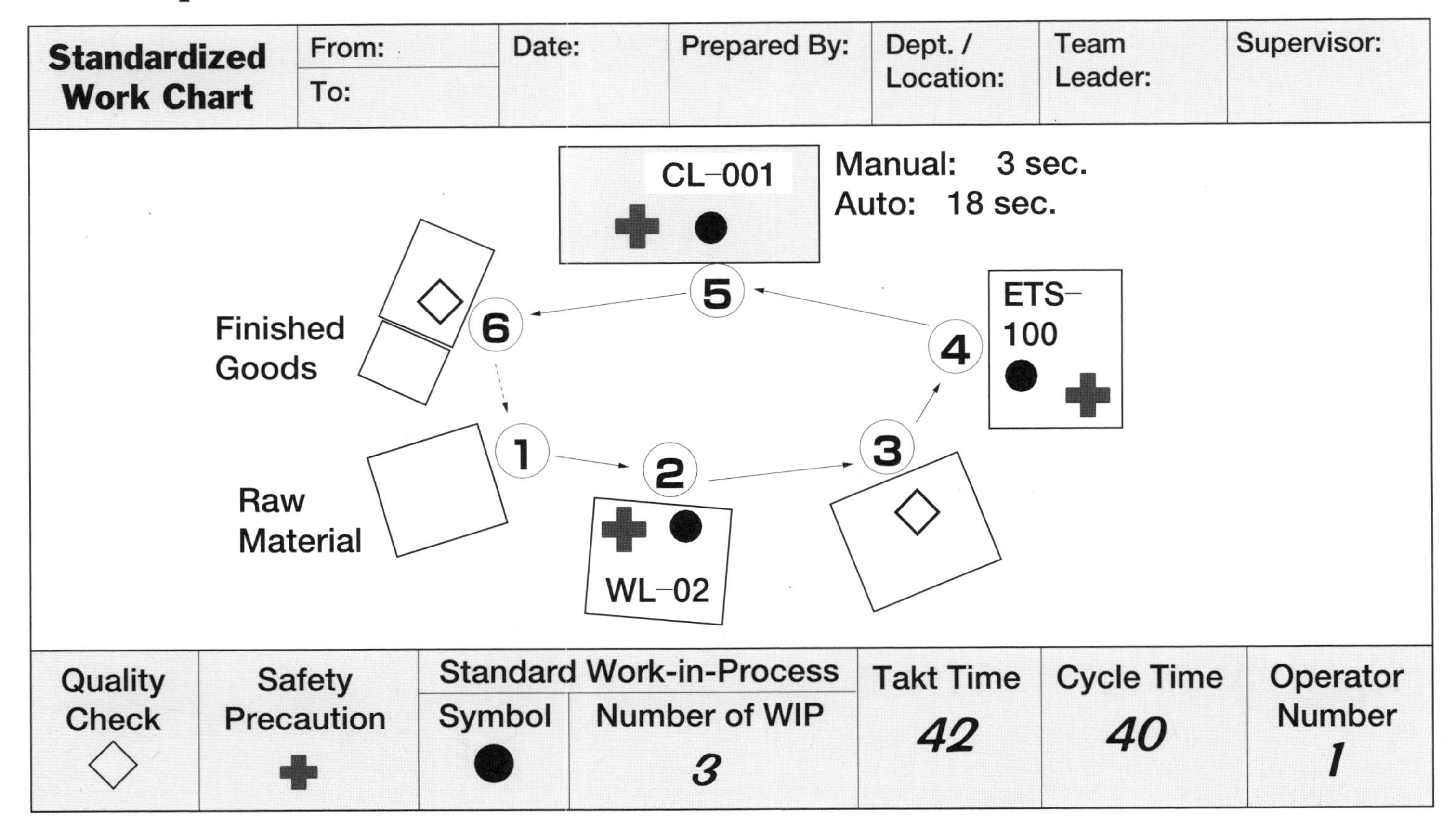

Standardized Work Chart	From: / To:	Date:	Prepared By:	Dept. / Location:	Team Leader:	Supervisor:

Quality Check	Safety Precaution	Standard Work-in-Process: Symbol	Standard Work-in-Process: Number of WIP	Takt Time	Cycle Time	Operator Number
◇	✚	●	3	42	40	1

The Standardized Work Chart shows operator movement and material location in relation to the machine and overall process layout. It should show takt time, cycle time, work sequence, and standard WIP.

標準作業票は、作業者の動きと部材の配置を設備と関連付けて表現し、工程全体のレイアウトがわかるようにするものです。タクトタイム、サイクルタイム、作業順序、標準手持ちは、必須です。

Standardized Work 4: Job Instruction Sheet (標準作業4: 標準作業指導書)

Job Instruction Sheet	Part # / Part Name	Required Quantity:	Date:	Dept. /Location: / Prepared By:	Team Leader:	Supervisor:

#	Step	Quality Check		Note	Time
		Sampling	Tool		
				Total	

Takt Time	Cycle Time	STD WIP	◇ Quality ✚ Safety ● STD WIP

Kaizen Express

Example of Job Instruction Sheet (標準作業指導書の例)

Job Instruction Sheet	Part # 26-0012	Required Quantity: 550	Date: April 26, 2007	Dept./Location:	Team Leader:	Supervisor:
	Part Name Base Unit Assembly			Prepared By:		

Takt Time	Cycle Time	STD WIP	◇ Quality ✚ Safety ● STD WIP
42	40	3	

#	Step	Quality Check		Note	Time
		Sampling	Tool		
1	*Get a work piece and set into fixture*			*With both left and right hand*	*1*
2	*Remove finished & set new one*				*2*
3	*Check appearance*	*1/1*	Slide Gauge		*12*
4	*Remove finished & set new one*			*Clean up head for every cycle*	*14*
5	*Remove finished & set new one*			*Ensure direction*	*3*
6	*Check appearance & put into container*	*1/1*	–	*Check both sides*	*8*
				Total	*40*

The Job Instruction Sheet is used to train new operators. It lists the steps of the job, detailing any special knack that may be required to perform the job safely with utmost quality and efficiency. It can also be useful for experienced operators to reconfirm the right operations.

標準作業指導書は、新人の訓練に用いるものです。作業手順を書き出し、安全に、良い品質のものを、効率的にこなすための注意点、つまり「急所」を記入します。ベテランの作業者にとっても、注意点を確認するのに役立ちます。

Skills Training Matrix (スキル管理板)

Skills Training Matrix	Can do generally	Certified	Factory Name:	Foreman:
	Can do well	Can do training	By:	Date Updated:

#	Operator Names	Processes														Current Date	Target Date

Kaizen Express

Example of Skills Training Matrix (スキル管理板の例)

Skills Training Matrix	Can do generally / Can do well	Certified / Can do training	Factory Name:	Foreman:
			By:	Date:

#	Operator	Processes: Cut	Bend	Grind	Weld	Test	Repair	Assem	M.Test	E.Test	Shipping	Current Date	Target Date
1	Mary Li				April/E	April/E	April/E	Aug./E	June/E	May/E	July/E		
2	Jerry Quan	Aug./E	Sept./E	May/E	May/E	June/E	July/E	April/E	April/E	April/E	April/E		
3	Sharron Ho	April/E	April/E	April/E	April/E	April/E	April/E						
	...												

The Skills Training Matrix shows the required and attained skills of every operator. The training schedule also should be shown.

スキル管理板は、それぞれの作業者について、必要なスキルと習得済みのスキルを表示するものです。訓練計画も明確にしなければなりません(多能工訓練予定表とも呼びます)。

プリント教材
Training Materials

１枚ずつのプリント教材を配布資料として活用して下さい。１枚ずつなら学びやすく、すぐに取り出して繰り返し確認することもできるでしょう。

We invite you to make copies of these one-page training materials to use as handouts. One-page lessons are easy to understand and convenient to keep for quick reference from time to time.

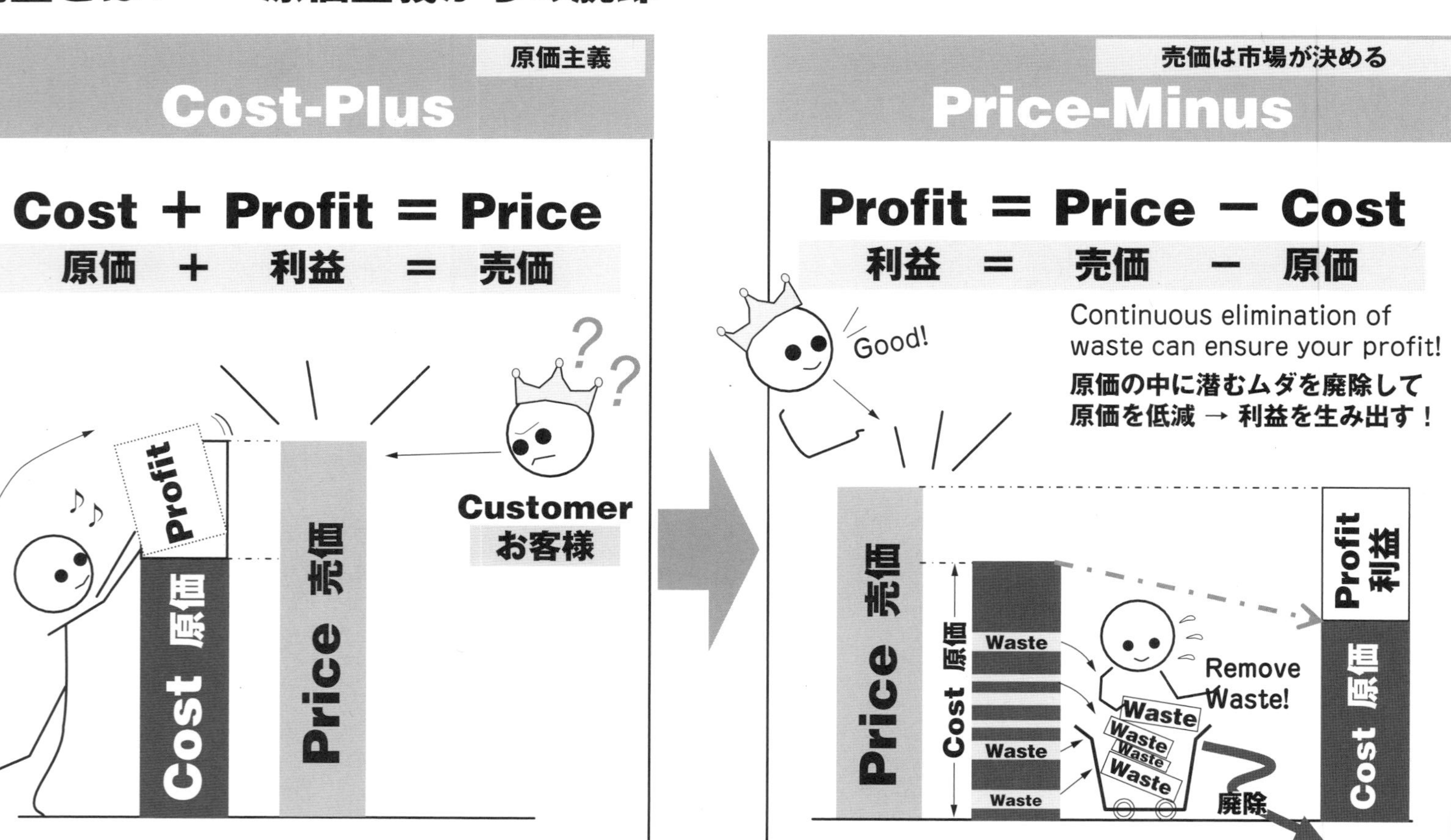
How Do You Make a Profit?
利益とは？　～原価主義からの脱却～
原価主義
Cost-Plus
Cost + Profit = Price
原価 + 利益 = 売価
Customer
お客様
Profit
Cost 原価
Price 売価
売価は市場が決める
Price-Minus
Profit = Price − Cost
利益 = 売価 − 原価
Continuous elimination of waste can ensure your profit!
原価の中に潜むムダを廃除して
原価を低減 → 利益を生み出す！
Good!
Price 売価
Cost 原価
Waste
Remove Waste!
廃除
Profit 利益
Cost 原価

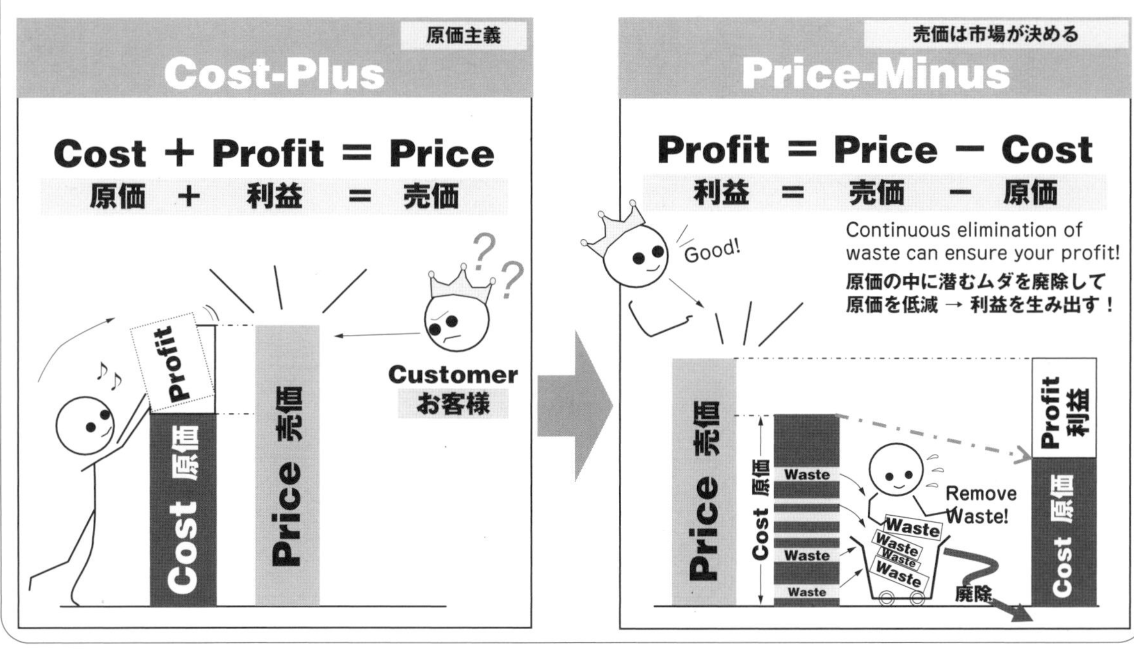

Kaizen Express

利益を出すには？

コストにマージンを乗せて利益を出しますか？それとも目標の売価を設定し、コストを低減することで利益を出しますか？

原価主義からの脱却

たとえば原価に30％の利益を上乗せして売価を決める。これが「原価主義」です。しかし、売価を決めるのは誰でしょう？　お客様ですか？　それとも私たちメーカーですか？

利益 ＝ 売価 − 原価

利益とは売価から原価を引いたものであって、決して、原価＋利益＝売価ではないのです。この2つの式は教室で習う数学では同じ意味かもしれませんが、私たちが働く人として利益を考える時、決して「同じではない」のです。

徹底したムダ廃除で原価低減

利益を得るには、原価の中に潜むムダを発見し、徹底的に廃除し続ける以外に方法はないのです。

How does your company ensure making a profit?

Do you add a margin on top of your cost to determine your profit? Or, do you set a target price and then reduce costs to ensure a profit?

Beyond cost-plus (cost + profit = price)

Setting the price by adding 30 (or any) percent to the cost is a kind of "Cost-Plus" philosophy. But, who should decide the price, our customer or us, the supplier?

Profit = price − cost

Price-minus thinking means that the profit is to be induced by subtracting the cost from the price. Mathematically, these are the same, but philosophically they are radically different and result in very different operational approaches.

Cost reduction through eliminating waste

We can truly guarantee that we get a profit only by continuous cost reduction through identifying and eliminating the waste that is hidden in the cost.

What Is Your Philosophy of Efficiency?　「能率」とは？

Apparent Efficiency vs. True Efficiency

見かけの能率と、真の能率

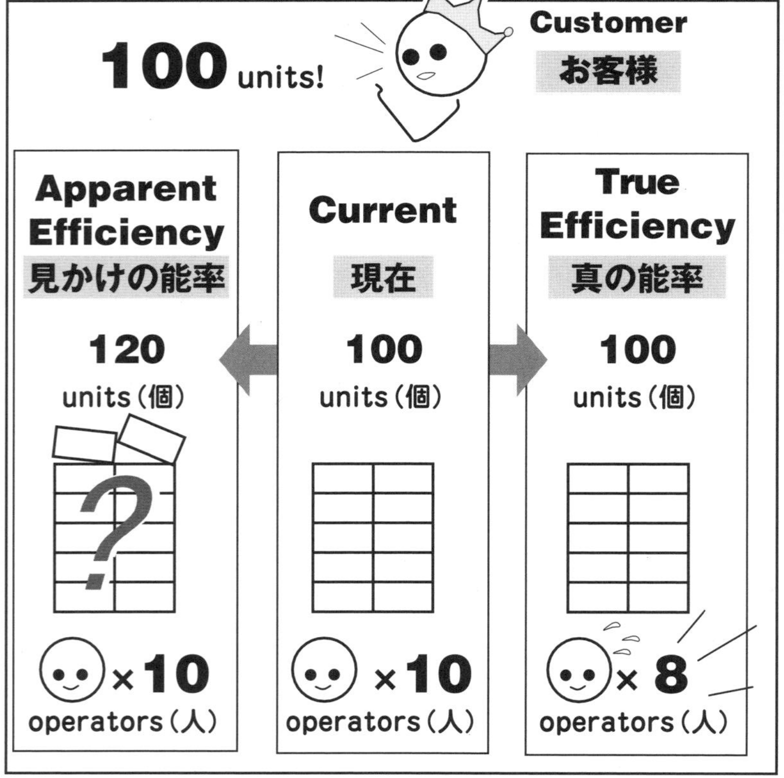

Customer
お客様

100 units!

Apparent Efficiency 見かけの能率	Current 現在	True Efficiency 真の能率
120 units（個）	100 units（個）	100 units（個）
×10 operators（人）	×10 operators（人）	× 8 operators（人）

Local Efficiency vs. Total Productivity

部分の能率と、全体の効率

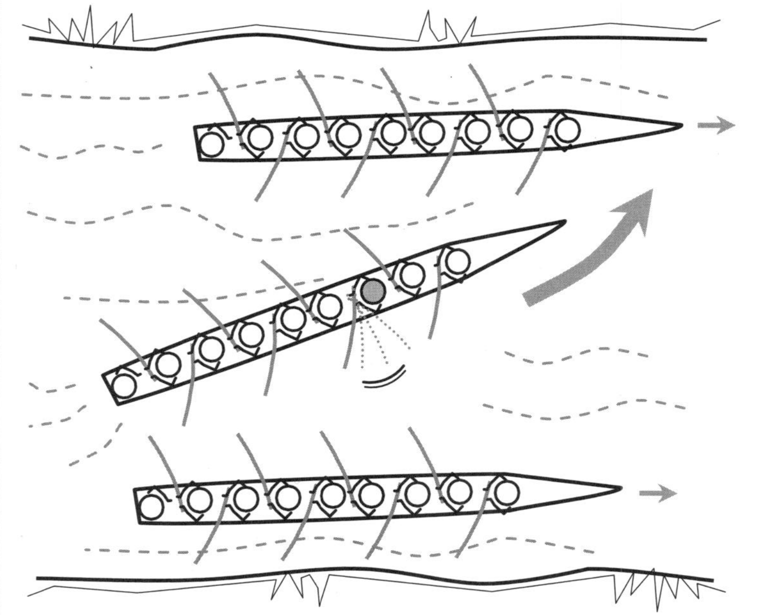

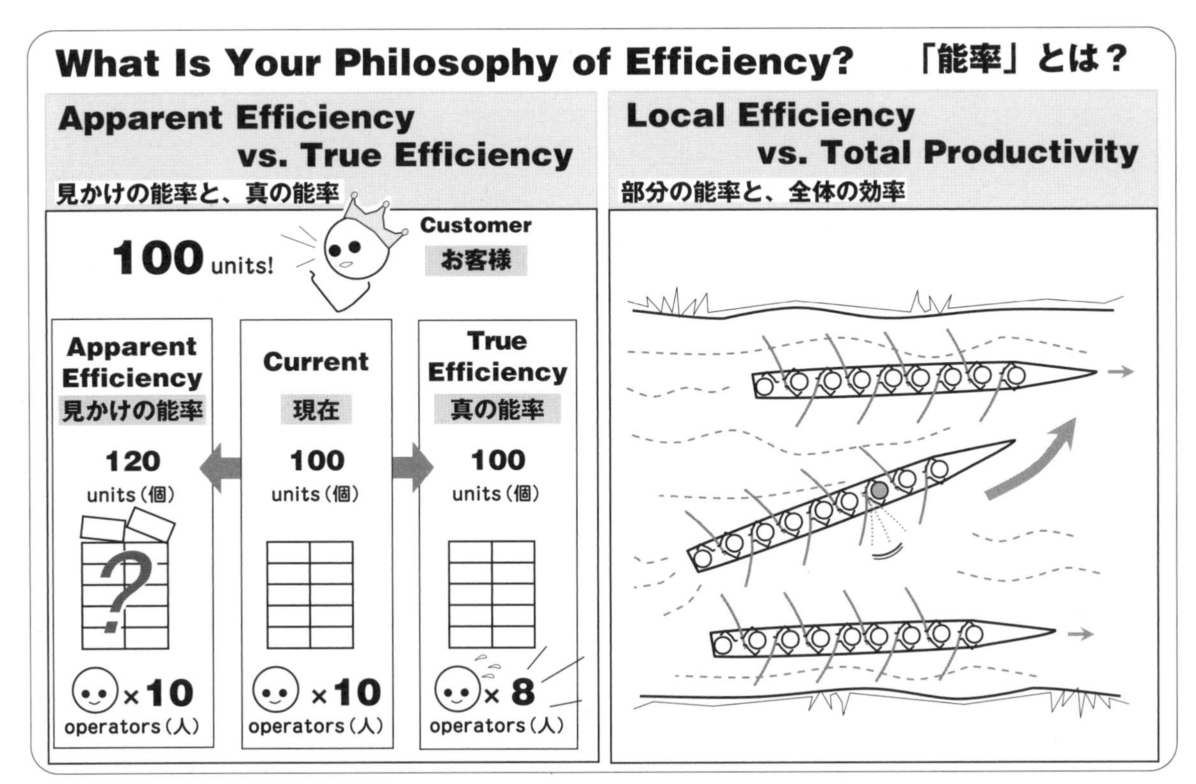

Kaizen Express

「能率」とは？

工程や人の「能率が良い」あるいは「能率が悪い」とあなたが言う時、それはどんな意味ですか？

What is your philosophy of efficiency?

What do you mean when you say that a process or person is working efficiently or inefficiently?

見かけの能率と、真の能率

お客様が100個欲しい時に、120個つくって20％の能率アップ。これは「見かけの能率」でしかありません。今10人なら、8人で100個つくれるようになることが、「真の能率」の改善なのです。

Apparent efficiency vs. true efficiency

Is it efficient to get a 20-percent increase by producing 120 units when the customer requires only 100 units? True efficiency is to produce the required 100 units with only eight operators when current methods require ten operators!

部分の能率と、全体の効率

図のまん中のボートはなぜまっすぐ進むことができないのでしょう？　ボートの例ならすぐにわかるのに、私たちは自分の現場の「部分の能率」だけを追い求めてしまいがちです。

Local efficiency vs. total productivity

Why is the middle boat not going straight? While we can easily understand the example of the boat, at work we tend to look simplistically for local efficiency rather than total productivity.

Overproduction: The Worst Form of Waste!
つくりすぎが最も悪いムダ!

I need 30 units of A
and 10 units of B!

Customer
お客様

Warehouse
倉庫

A
B
?
C
?

Kaizen Express

つくりすぎに気付こう！

図をじっと見て下さい。どんなムダがありますか？　つくりすぎとは何か、皆で話し合ってみましょう。

Can you see overproduction?

Look at the chart above. What type of waste

do you see? Talk together about the waste of overproduction!

つくりすぎが問題を覆い隠す

つくりすぎが覆い隠してしまう問題とは何ですか？

Overproduction makes you blind

What kind of problems do you think might be concealed by overproduction?

つくりすぎをやめたらどうなる？

つくりすぎをやめたら、次の観点から見て、どんなインパクトがあるでしょう？

—品質は？
—コストは？
—後工程のお客様から見ると？
—自工程の作業者にとっては？
—自工程の監督者にとっては？

What results occur if you stop overproducing?

What impact does preventing overproduction have on the follow items?

—What about quality?
—What about cost reduction?
—What does it mean to the customer downstream?
—How does it impact the operators?
—How does it change what the Team Leaders do?

Lead Time: Focus Your Eyes on Stagnating Time Rather than Processing Time!
リードタイム短縮は、加工時間よりも停滞時間に目を向ける！

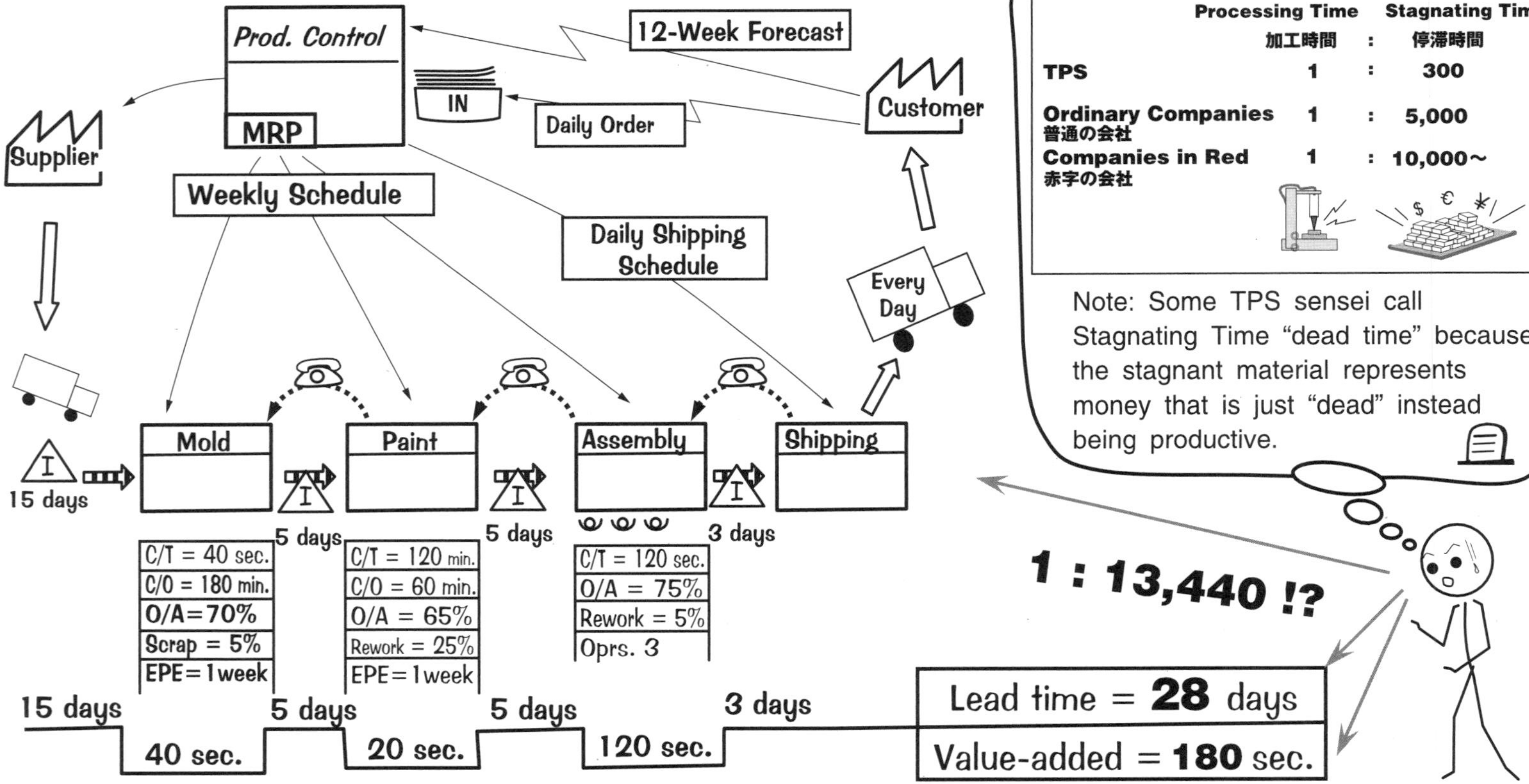

	Processing Time 加工時間	:	Stagnating Time 停滞時間
TPS	1	:	300
Ordinary Companies 普通の会社	1	:	5,000
Companies in Red 赤字の会社	1	:	10,000～

Note: Some TPS sensei call Stagnating Time "dead time" because the stagnant material represents money that is just "dead" instead being productive.

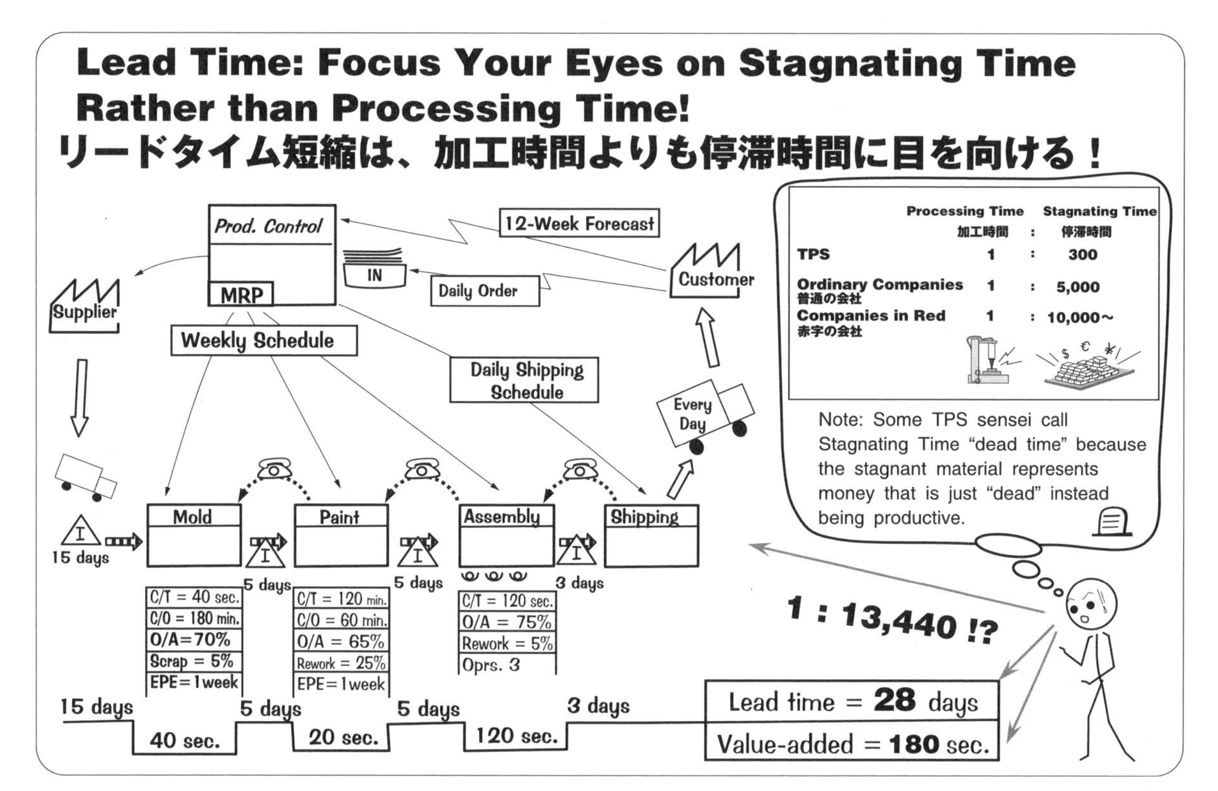

Kaizen Express

加工時間と停滞時間を比べてみれば？！

リードタイムとは、

リードタイム ＝ 加工時間 ＋ 停滞時間

であると言うことができます。

あなたの会社、あなたの生産ラインのリードタイムはどのくらいですか？ 加工時間と停滞時間の比率はどのくらいでしょう？

実際に付加価値を付けている加工時間より、加工されるのを待っているだけの停滞時間のほうがずっと長いことに気付くでしょう。

リードタイムを短縮するには？

したがって、リードタイムを短縮するには、加工時間そのものを短縮しようとするよりも、圧倒的に長い停滞の時間を短縮したほうが、より早く、より大きな効果が得られるのです。

なぜ停滞するのか？

モノの流れが切れているところには必ず停滞があり、停滞があれば積み替えや運搬が必要になります。

Compare processing time and stagnating time!

Lead Time ＝ processing ＋ stagnating

How long is the lead time of the product produced on your production line? Of that time, how much is processing time vs. stagnating time?

Usually, much more time is spent stagnating — parts being accumulated before being sent to next process — than being processed.

What should we do to shorten our lead time?

Therefore, we can get a better result quicker by shortening the stagnating time rather than trying to reduce the processing time.

Why do things stagnate?

We have some accumulation everywhere the flow of product is interrupted and we have to load/unload and convey those items to the following processes.

Manpower: Distinguish Value-Creating Work from Just Moving!
工数削減のポイントは、動きと働きの違いに着目！

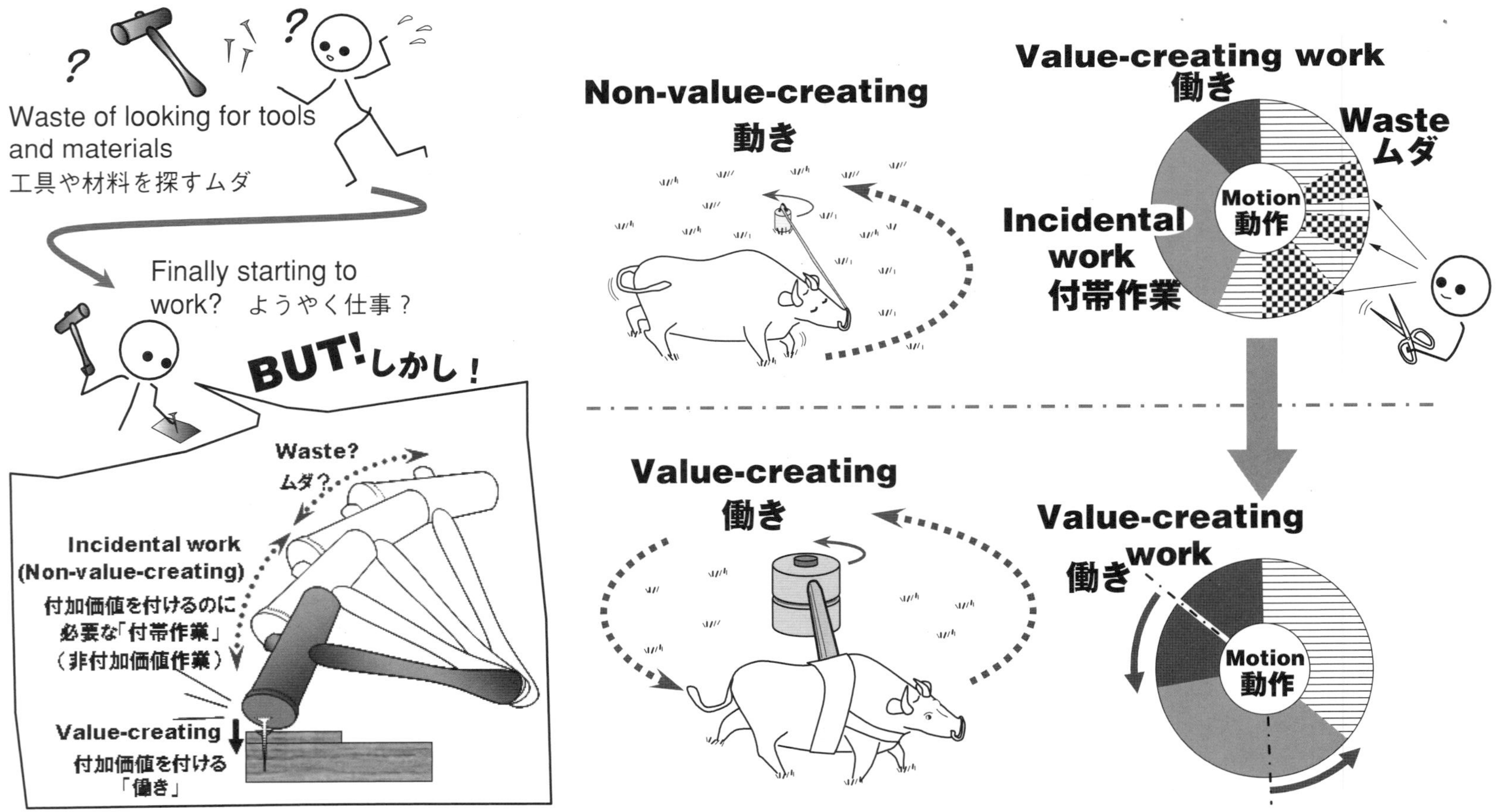

Waste of looking for tools and materials
工具や材料を探すムダ

Finally starting to work?　ようやく仕事？

BUT! しかし！

Waste?
ムダ？

Incidental work
(Non-value-creating)
付加価値を付けるのに
必要な「付帯作業」
（非付加価値作業）

Value-creating
付加価値を付ける
「働き」

Non-value-creating
動き

Value-creating work
働き

Waste
ムダ

Motion
動作

Incidental work
付帯作業

Value-creating
働き

Value-creating work
働き

Motion
動作

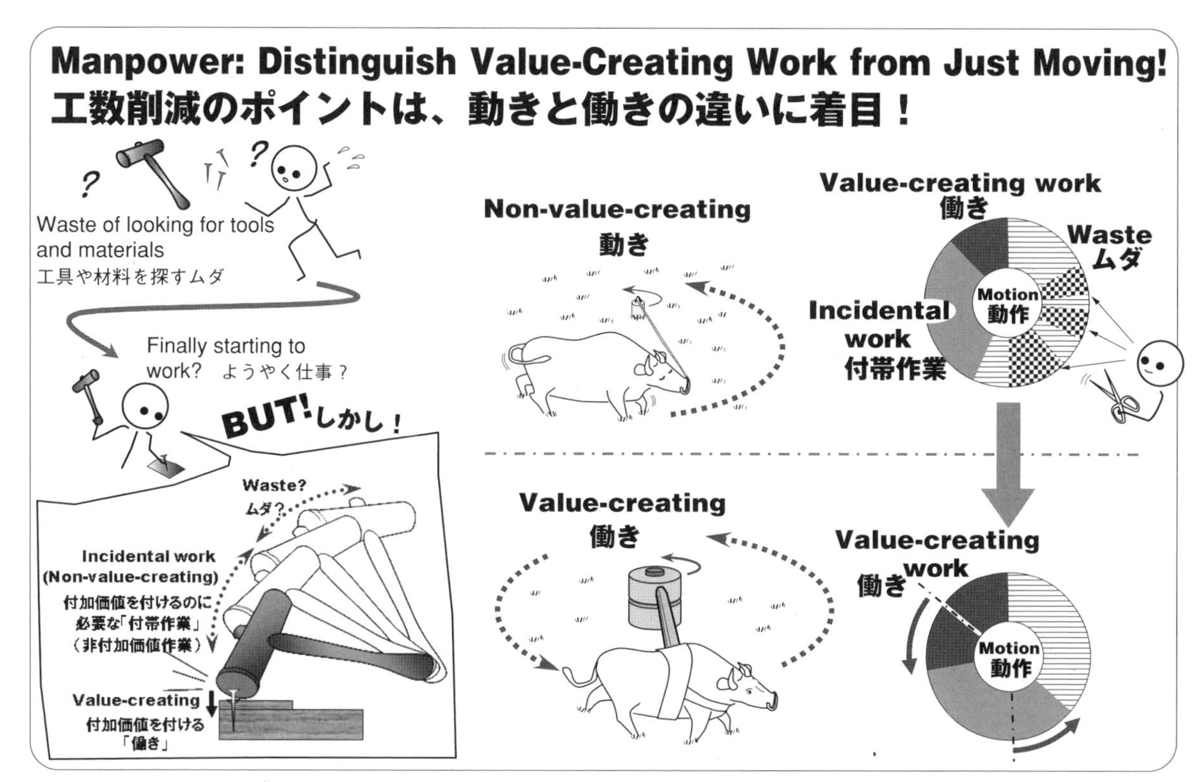

Kaizen Express

「働く」とは？

トヨタでは、「働く」とは工程が進み、仕事が出来上がること、とされています。単に「動いて」いるだけではいけないのはもちろん、価値を生み出しながら「工程が進む」ことが不可欠です。皆さんの現場では、どうですか？　「動き」を「働き」に変える改善ができていますか？

付加価値を付けている時間はとても短い?!

たとえば、金槌で釘を打つ時、本当に付加価値を付けているのは、釘が板にめり込む瞬間だけです。

動きと働きの違いに気付こう！

あなたの毎日のすべての仕事を、単なる「動き」と付加価値を付けている「働き」に分けてみましょう。

動きを働きに変える

改善とは、労働強化ではなく、ムダを廃除して単なる動きを働きに変え、人の付加価値を高めることです。

What is work?

In TPS, we think of "work" as only those steps that directly create value. Simply moving is not creating value. How about your gemba? Is your kaizen converting "moving" to "working"?

Actual value-creating time is very short!!

For example, when hammering a nail, the value-creating time is only precisely the instant that the nail is hammered into the board.

Distinguishing work from movement is the first step to eliminate waste!

Separate all of your daily tasks into "movement" and "work."

Convert movement to "work."

Kaizen does not mean the intensification of labor but the conversion of movement to work so all of people's labor can be utilized to create value.

Machines: Do Flow and Motion Kaizen Before Machine Kaizen!
設備改善の前にまず工程改善、作業改善！

Isolated processes
工程と工程の間が離れている

Flow and motion kaizen
工程改善、作業改善

Machine kaizen
設備改善

Focus directly on the value-creating process
付加価値プロセスに着目

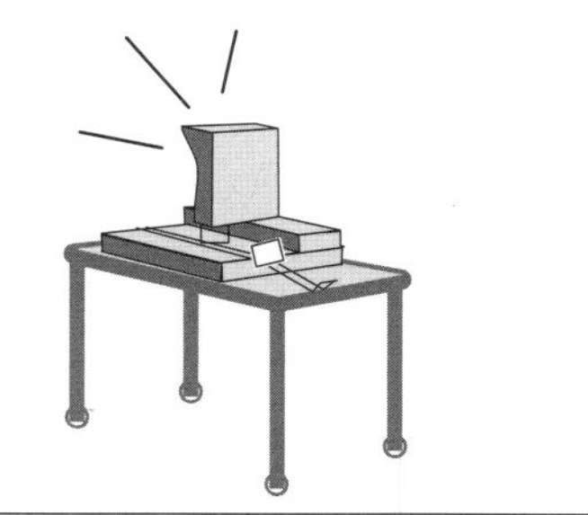

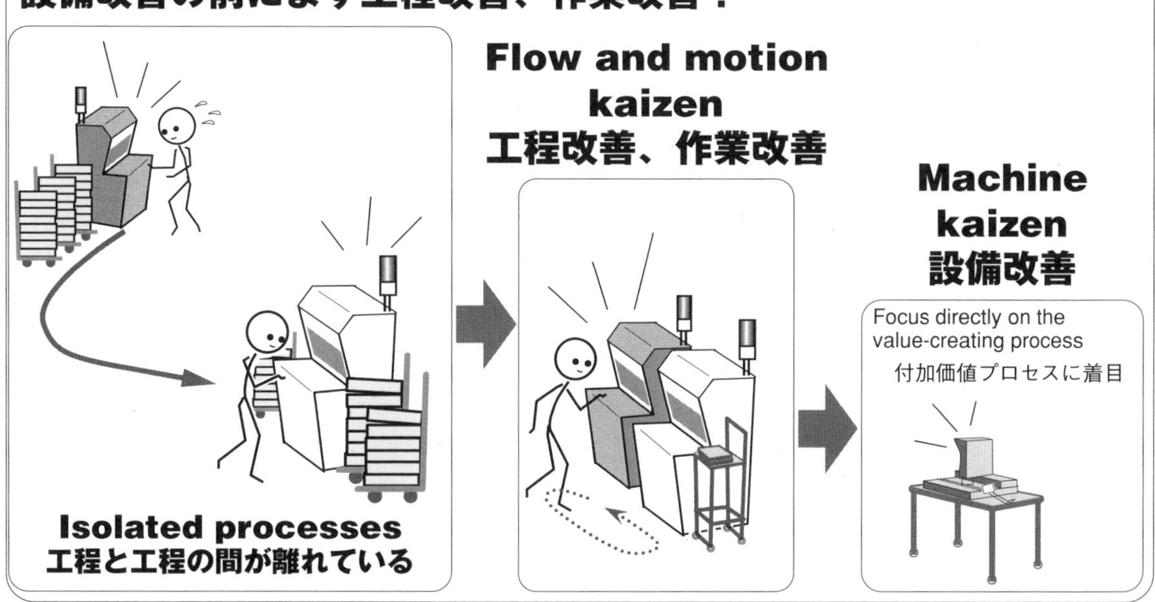

Kaizen Express

設備改善はいつ、どのように？

設備改善は非常に重要です。品質や生産性の大幅な改善につながり、また作業者のムリを減らすこともできるでしょう。しかし、設備改善は難しく、また高価なものになってしまう可能性もあります。さらに、設備はモノの流れと人の働きを支えるものでなければなりません。ですから、私たちは、工程改善と作業改善を徹底的に追求した後で設備改善に取り掛かるべきなのです。

When do you pursue machine kaizen?

Machine kaizen is very important and can lead to big improvements in quality and productivity and can reduce muri for workers. But, it can also be difficult and expensive. And machines should be configured to support the flow of product and the work of operators. Therefore, we only pursue machine kaizen AFTER doing flow and motion kaizen.

まずは設備を工程順に並べるべし！

離れ小島をなくそう！　離れ小島はムダの元、離れ小島があると、改善が難しくなってしまうのです。

Line up machines in a sequential flow

Eliminate isolated islands! Isolated islands always cause waste and make it hard to do kaizen.

Quality: Inspect Products One-by-One Immediately at the Source Process!

「つくったところですぐ検査！」が製造不良ゼロへの道！

- Where and when? - いつどこでつくったか？
- Who made it? - 誰が不良をつくったか？
- How and why? - どうやって、なぜ？

With overproduction and large inventories, you can never spot defects immediately!

不良をつくってしまっても、検査するまでわからない！

Quality: Inspect Products One-by-One Immediately at the Source Process!
「つくったところですぐ検査！」が製造不良ゼロへの道！

- Where and when? - いつどこでつくったか？
- Who made it? - 誰が不良をつくったか？
- How and why? - どうやって、なぜ？

With overproduction and large inventories, you can never spot defects immediately!
不良をつくってしまっても、検査するまでわからない！

Every worker is an inspector!
すべての作業者は検査員！

Never
-accept,
-build, or
-pass on
a defect!!

不良は、1つも
- 受け取らない
- つくらない
- 後工程へ流さない！！

Kaizen Express

不良について話し合ってみましょう

— どれだけ早く不良を発見できますか？
— 品質のつくり込みに責任を持つべき人は誰ですか？
— お客様への品質保証はどうやって実現しますか？
— すばやい問題発見と対応をどのように実現しますか？

Talk together about your defects!

— How quickly can you spot defects in your workplace?
— Who is responsible for building in quality?
— How do you ensure perfect quality to the customer?
— How does your work site identify and respond to problems?

分業の最終検査の問題点

最終検査を分業で行っていたのでは、不良を即座に発見することは非常に困難です。また、真因の追究もなかなかできません。それに、製品が最終検査工程に届くまでの間にも、同じ種類の不良をたくさんつくってしまっているかもしれないのです！

Problems of final inspection

It is very hard to find defects immediately by final inspection. It is also difficult to identify the root cause. And by the time the product reaches final inspection, we may have produced many of the same defects!

自工程品質保証を確立しよう！

つくった工程で品質をつくり込み、検査するのなら、不良の発見も、真因の特定も、ずっと簡単にできるようになります。

Ensure your quality at the source process!

It is much easier to find defects and identify their root causes if we build in and inspect quality at each source process.

ワードリスト&索引
Word List & Index

本書では、ヘボン式に若干の変更を加えた表記法を用います。ヘボン式とは、ローマン(つまりラテン語の)・アルファベットを用いて日本語を書き表そうとするとき、最もよく使われる一般的な表記法で、日本語では「ローマ字」(ローマの文字の意)と呼ばれます。

Kaizen Express uses a revised Hepburn system, the first and most common method to write Japanese using the Roman (or Latin) alphabet, called "romaji" ("Roman letters") in Japanese.

ワードリスト&索引　Word List & Index

さ Sa (Sa, Shi / Si, Su, Se, So / Za, Zi, Zu, Ze, Zo)

な Na (Na, Ni, Nu, Ne, No)

は Ha (Ha, Hi, Hu (Fu), He, Ho / Pa, Pi, Pu, Pe, Po / Ba, Bi, Bu, Be, Bo)

日本語 Japanese [Nihongo]	英語 English [Eigo]	参照ページ Pages
離れ小島 [hanare kojima]	isolated island (isolated process)	25
ハネ出し [hanedashi]	auto-eject	61, 73, 75-77
反時計回り [han tokei mawari]	counterclockwise	35
日当たり平均所要 [hiatari heikin shoyō]	average daily demand	18
引き取り [hikitori]	pull or withdrawal	26
引き取りかんばん [hikitori kanban]	withdrawal kanban	38, 39
ピッチ [picchi]	pitch	34
必要なものを、必要なときに、必要なだけつくり、提供する [hitsuyō na mono wo, hitsuyō na toki ni, hitsuyō na dake tsukuri, teikyō suru]	making and delivering what is needed, just when it is needed, and just in the amount needed	16
人の仕事と機械の仕事を分ける [hito no shigoto to kikai no shigoto wo wakeru]	separating human work and machine work	72
一人完結 [hitori kanketsu]	produce with only one operator; only one operator makes the product from beginning to end	25
人を尊重する [hito wo sonchō suru]	respecting people	107
ひもスイッチ [himo suicchi (switch)]	signal cord	52, 81, 82
標準作業 [hyōjun sagyō]	standardized work	84
標準作業組み合わせ票 [hyōjun sagyō kumiawase hyō]	Standardized Work Combination Table	85, 118-119
標準作業指導書 [hyōjun sagyō shidō sho]	Job Instruction Sheet	85, 122-123
標準作業票 [hyōjun sagyō hyō]	Standardized Work Chart	85, 120-121
標準手持ち [hyōjun temochi]	standard in-process stock, or standard WIP	84
フォード式 [fōdo shiki]	Fordism	21-22
付加価値を生まない作業 [fukakachi wo umanai sagyō]	non-value-creating work	3, 134-137
付加価値をつける働き [fukakachi wo tsukeru hataraki]	value-creating work	3, 134-137
付帯作業 [futai sagyō]	incidental work	3, 136-137
部品の置き方 [buhin no okikata]	parts presentation	35, 91
不良ゼロ [furyō zero]	zero defects	80, 140-141
不良をつくるムダ [furyō wo tsukuru muda]	waste of correction, waste of defects	3
分業型レイアウト [bungyō gata reiauto (layout)]	process village layout, or job shop layout	23
平準化 [heijunka]	heijunka	17, 43
ペースメーカー [peisu meikah (pacemaker)]	pacemaker	47, 48
可動率 [bekidōritsu, or kadōritsu]	operational availability	51, 62

カイゼン・エクスプレス
日本語　書き方&読み方ガイド

ローマ字を使った日本語の書き方と読み方の表現

本書では、ヘボン式に若干の変更を加えた表記法を用います。ヘボン式とは、ローマン(つまりラテン語の)・アルファベットを用いて日本語を書き表そうとするとき、最もよく使われる一般的な表記法で、日本語では「ローマ字」(ローマの文字の意)と呼ばれます。

日本語の発音

1. ほとんどすべての音節は母音で終わります。唯一の例外は、"ん(*N*)"で終わるもの。
2. 母音は常に同じように発音されます。母音は単独で使われ、二重母音はありません。
3. 子音である"*R*"音は巻き舌で1回 (スペイン語やイタリア語の"*R*"は複数の巻き舌音ですが、それらの言語における"*R*"の発音とは異なります)。

日本語の母音は次の5つ：

A	as in "c**a**r," not "c**a**n"
I	as in "id**i**ot," not "**i**diot"
U	as in "b**oo**t," not "b**u**t"
E	as in "b**e**t," not "b**e**at"
O	as in "n**o**," not "n**o**t"

日本語では、単音の母音と長音母音をはっきり区別して使うことが大切です。本書では、ヘボン式に若干の変更を加えて、長母音を次のように紹介します。：

A	ah	(あー)
I	ii	(いー)
U	ū	(うー)
E	ei	(えい)
O	ō	(おー)

例外

大野耐一先生の「おおの」は、すでに世界中で"Ohno"という表現が一般的になっていることから、本書でも"Ōno"ではなく、"Ohno"を使います。

Kaizen Express
Guide to Writing and Pronouncing Japanese

Romanization

Kaizen Express uses a slightly revised Hepburn system, the first and most common method to write Japanese using the Roman (or Latin) alphabet, called "romaji" ("Roman letters") in Japanese.

Pronunciation

1. Almost all syllables end in a vowel. The only exception is that some end in "*N*."
2. All vowels are pronounced the same, every time. Simple vowels only, no diphthongs.
3. The consonant represented by the letter "*R*" is trilled once (not unlike the trill of a Spanish or Italian "*R*" although those languages usually trill "*R*" more than once).

The five Japanese vowels are:

A as in "c**a**r," not "c**a**n"
I as in "idi**o**t," not "**i**diot"
U as in "b**oo**t," not "b**u**t"
E as in "b**e**t," not "b**e**at"
O as in "n**o**," not "n**o**t"

An important distinction is made in Japanese between long and short vowels. Long vowels are shown in the *Kaizen Express* revised Hepburn system as follows:

A ah
I ii
U ū
E ei
O ō

Exception

Words that are commonly known in English will follow the common spelling. So, "Ohno" Taiichi will remain "Ohno," not "Ōno."

Word List & Index

T

U

参考文献
Bibliography

※日本の書籍は、本書発行時点で英訳本が存在するものを紹介しています。
*As for TPS books in the Japanese language, we introduce the following books that had been translated into English at the time when *Kaizen Express* was published.

- 大野耐一、1978年、トヨタ生産方式―脱規模の経営をめざして、ダイヤモンド社
  Ohno, Taiichi, 1988. *Toyota Production System: Beyond Large-Scale Production.* Productivity Press.

- 大野耐一、2001年(1983年版の新装版)、大野耐一の現場経営、日本能率協会マネジメントセンター
  Ohno, Taiichi, 1988. *Workplace Management.* Productivity Press.
  2001年新装版の英訳本は下記にて入手可。
  The latest translation is the 2007 translation by Jon Miller, Gemba Press (only available in the Kaizen Products Store at http://gembapress.com/).

- Harris, Rick, Harris, Chris, and Wilson, Earl. 2003. *Making Materials Flow.* Lean Enterprise Institute.

- Marchwinski, Chet, and Shook, John, compilers. 2006. *Lean Lexicon (Third Edition).* Lean Enterprise Institute.

- Rother, Mike, and Shook, John. 1998. *Learning to See.* Lean Enterprise Institute.
  トヨタ生産方式にもとづく「モノ」と「情報」の流れ図で現場の見方を変えよう!!
  2001年8月　日刊工業新聞社

- Rother, Mike, and Harris, Rick, 2001. *Creating Continuous Flow.* Lean Enterprise Institute.

- Smalley, Art. 2004. *Creating Level Pull.* Lean Enterprise Institute.
  トヨタ生産方式にもとづく『ちょろ引き』で生産管理を改革しよう!!
  2006年10月　日刊工業新聞社

- Womack, James, and Jones, Daniel, 1996. *Lean Thinking.* Simon & Schuster.
  リーン・シンキング、稲垣公夫訳(「ムダなし企業への挑戦」の改題)
  1997年6月　日経BP社(2003年改題)

- Womack, James, and Jones, Daniel, 2002. *Seeing the Whole.* Lean Enterprise Institute.

著者紹介
About the Authors

成沢　俊子 (なるさわ　としこ)

1983年～2002年NECに勤務。金融庁勤務を経て、PEC産業教育センターにて改善を研究。人間環境大学非常勤講師。"Learning to See"「トヨタ生産方式にもとづく『モノ』と『情報』の流れ図で現場の見方を変えよう!!」(2001)、"Creating Level Pull"「トヨタ生産方式にもとづく『ちょろ引き』で生産管理を改革しよう!!」(2006)（ともに日刊工業新聞社）の翻訳者。

John Shook (ジョン・シュック)

Lean Enterprise Institute シニア・アドバイザー。TWI Network, Inc.代表、Lean Transformation, LLC.代表。ミシガン大学Japan Technology Management Program 前Director。1983年、最初の外国人正規社員としてトヨタ本社に入社、後にトヨタ本社初の米国人課長となる。Toyota North American engineering & R&D center総務部長、Toyota Supplier Support Center副所長を経て、現職。主な著書に "Learning to See"、"Managing to Learn" 他。

Toshiko Narusawa (成沢　俊子)

Toshiko learned about the Toyota Production System as a kaizen leader for the Japanese electronics company NEC where she worked from 1983 to 2002. After leaving NEC, she worked for the Financial Service Agency of Japan, where she and her team developed a risk-monitoring system to cope with the Japanese banking crisis, and then worked as a kaizen instructor for PEC (Personal Education Center, a consulting firm in Japan headed by Hitoshi Yamada). She has translated two books—*Learning To See* and *Creating Level Pull*—into Japanese and authored a popular series of articles for the Japanese periodical *Kojo Kanri* ("*Factory Management*"). Toshiko has supported kaizen at the gemba of many companies in Japan, China, and Southeast Asia. She continues to enjoy learning about practical kaizen while working with gemba people.

John Shook (ジョン　シュック)

John learned about lean while working for Toyota Motor Corporation—where he became the company's first American "kacho" (manager) in Japan—from 1983 to 1994, helping that company transfer the Toyota ways of production, product development, and management from Japan to its affiliated overseas companies and suppliers. After leaving Toyota, John taught industrial engineering at the University of Michigan where he was also director of the Japan Technology Management Program. Currently, John is a senior advisor for the Lean Enterprise Institute and heads two consulting groups, the Lean Transformations Group LLC, and the TWI Network Inc. Author of *Managing to Learn* and co-author of *Learning to See*, John works and learns with companies and individuals who wish to improve their operations and transform the way they manage.

23514